Vital Karate

Masutatsu Oyama

WARD LOCK LIMITED
LONDON

Photographers
Akira Kotani
Ihei Misaki

Japan Publications Trading Company
of San Francisco, and Tokyo
with editorial offices at
2-1, Sarugaku-cho 1-chome, Chiyoda-ku, Tokyo, Japan

ISBN 0 7063 1787 4
First British edition, September 1973. Reprinted, May 1974, January 1975.
Jointly published by
WARD LOCK LIMITED, Warwick House, 116 Baker Street,
London W1M 2BB

Layout and typography by Iwao Yoshizaki and Toshihiro Kuwahara
Made and printed in Japan by Dai Nippon Printing Co., Ltd.

preface

I feel sure that in the past years karate has grown in popularity more than any other sport both because of its terrific power and because mankind today, recognizing its hopeless spiritual situation, finds the answer to that problem in following the karate way. After spending three decades searching out the deepest meanings of karate, I have come to regard the dissemination of the true way my heaven-sent mission.

Feeling this way, I decided that writing books on the true karate would be the most efficient and effective way to achieve my aim. My first work, What is Karate?, *received tremendous approval. In 1965, after five years of hard work, I finished* This is Karate, *in response to the urgent demands of karate fans and instructors all over the world.*

Letters continued to pour into my office, even after the completion of these two books, requesting complete information on the highly sophisticated tameshiwari *breaking techniques and free-style practice fighting. I am happy to announce that thorough explanations of these and other specialist techniques will appear in a forthcoming volume entitled* Advanced Karate.

On the other hand, shortly after the publication of my other two books, I began receiving numerous requests for a concise clear karate manual designed especially for self-study. Vital Karate, *though limited in size, is the answer to those requests. Of course, it would be nearly impossible to cover the entire heart of karate in this little book, but we have given preeminence to the actual techniques and have included a practical text that explains all of the essentials.*

We have also included those that we thought would be most easily used in actual combat. A person who masters everything in this book should have considerable power. It will make me very happy if Vital Karate *can be of help in studying correct karate and in making your daily life happier and more meaningful.*

March, 1967 *Masutatsu Oyama*

contents

Always more vital to karate than techniques or strength is the spiritual element that lets you move and act with complete freedom. In striving to enter the proper frame of mind Zen meditation is of great importance. Though we say that this meditation involves a state of impassivity and complete lack of thought, we mean that through meditation we can overcome emotion and thinking and give freer reign to our innate abilities than ever before. The Zen state of selflessness is the same condition of disregard for selfish thoughts and concern for personal welfare that the artist experiences in the heart of creation. The man who wants to walk the way of karate cannot afford to neglect Zen and spiritual training.

Practice fighting is your best chance to put the basic elements you have learned into real action. Always bear two things in mind: you must approach practice fighting with the true martial-arts attitude of respecting what your opponent can do, and you must always strive to put what you know to best use.

Practice fighting demands that you bring together all that you have learned in daily training and that you crystalize your constant efforts to perfect your speed, strength, balance, and timing.

Practice fighting

When you try the speed and strength your daily training has given you in breaking boards, tiles, or bricks, you are doing more than just measuring your own ability; you are also giving yourself a chance to reflect on the effects your training has had on both your mind and your body. When you see for yourself that you can break these objects, you know that your body is possessed of the speed and strength you were striving for. A karate that ignores breaking practice is no more useful than a fruit tree that bears no fruit.

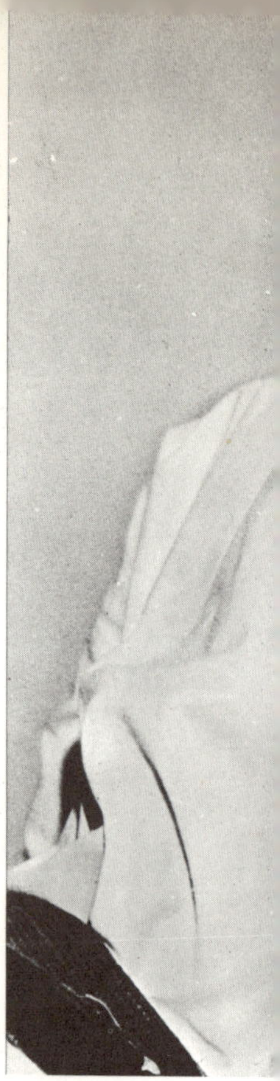

The breaking techniques permit a spiritually unified and trained man to exhibit feats of marvelous strength that the ordinary man cannot imagine. These photographs give an idea of the type of things a trained karate man can do, for instance, break a stack of 20 roofing tiles, chop the top off a standing beer bottle with his bare hand, throw a watermelon into the air and thrust his hand through it as it descends, or break three one-inch boards with the elbow.

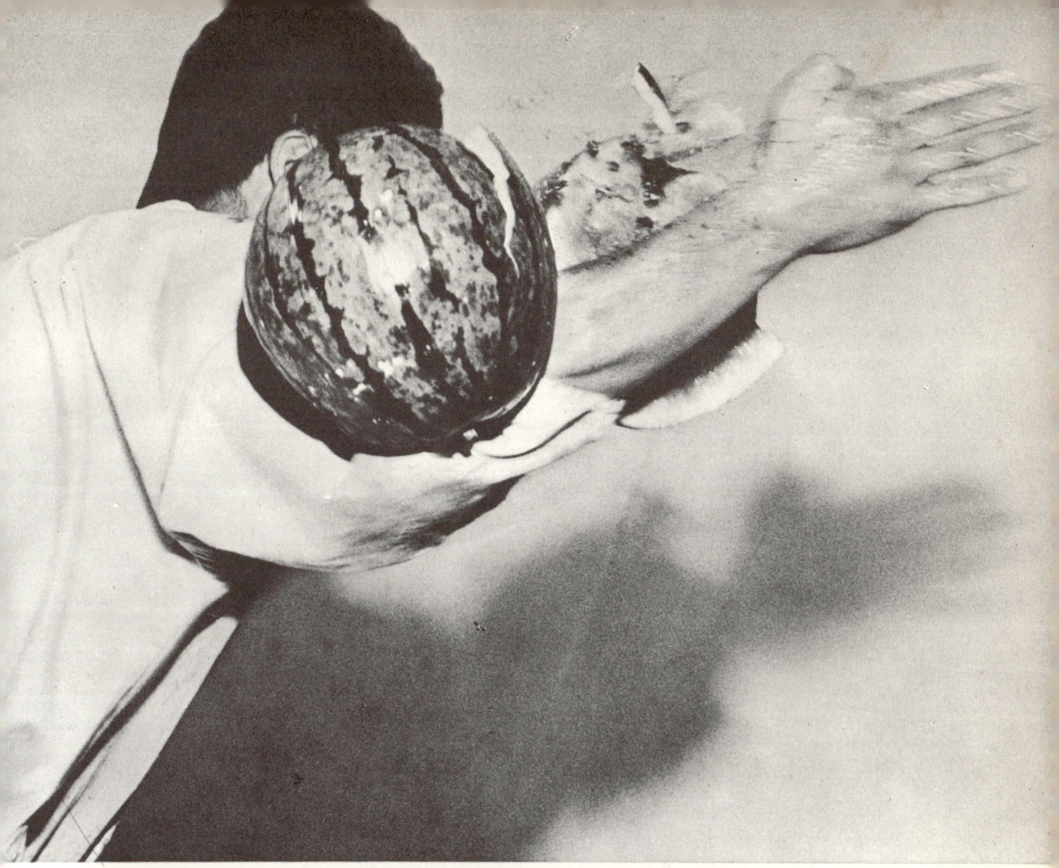

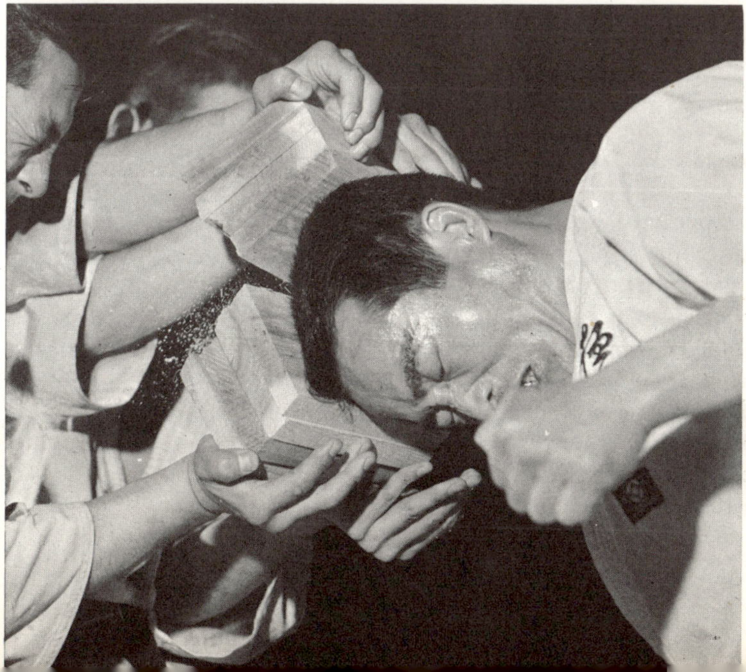

CHAPTER 1 karate weapons

Since karate is literally what the name means, fighting with empty hands, it demands that we transform the whole human body into a weapon and use it effectively. To reach the stage where it is possible to use all parts of the body, down to one single finger, as a powerful weapon, we must know the proper way to handle our bodies.

Since olden times, it has been said that the karate grip requires three years to learn, the standing method another three years, and the thrusting method still another three. In other words, making a powerful weapon of the body is the most important of all karate basics. Completely and correctly mastering this basic requires intensive training, and, as I tell all of my students, the very act of mastering it is the road to an understanding of karate's inner essence.

An old Japanese proverb used to show the deepest meaning of the Japanese military art of fencing (*kendo*) says, "If the sword is true, the heart is true; and if the heart is true, the sword is true." In the sense that the heart of the man who holds the sword is manifest in the sword itself, this maxim applies to karate where the weapon that replaces the *kendo* sword is the human body. For this reason, the karate man must take proper and good care of his body. I emphasize the care and training of the body to all beginning students because the body as a weapon is so vital to karate. All students must learn how to care for their bodies and must understand how to make of their bodies accurate and powerful karate weapons.

1. principle weapons : hands

In my long experience I have noticed that a large number of beginners entertain some highly mistaken ideas. For instance, many are under the grave misconception that in the fist and knife hand it is sufficient to strengthen only the skin and flesh of the striking area. This is completely wrong, of course, since without the cooperation of the wrist, arm, elbow, and shoulder the fist or the knife hand completely lack the destructive force of a weapon. You must always remember that logical training of the entire body and correct coordination of all the body parts are essential to the development of effective karate weapons.

how to make a proper fist

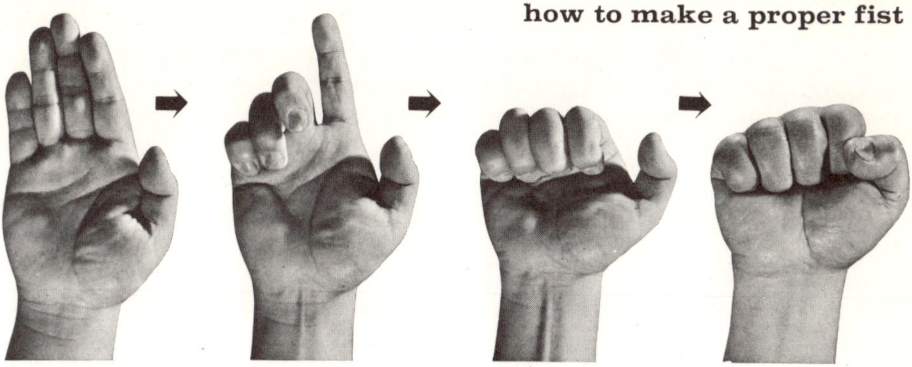

forefist ***(seiken)***

To grip your hand into a proper forefist, the most frequently used and important of the karate weapon positions, fold all four of your fingers in as tight as you can, and clamp your thumb down on top of them hard. By folding your fingers in firmly you both protect the joints at the fingers' bases and give tension to your wrist. Pay particular attention to the little finger, which has the tendency to dangle and separate from the fist.

The striking edge, or the part of the forefist that contacts the object to be struck, is the most important area. We always strike with what is called the head of the fist (*ken-to*), that is, the base knuckles of the forefinger and middle finger. This is the basic theory of the forefist.

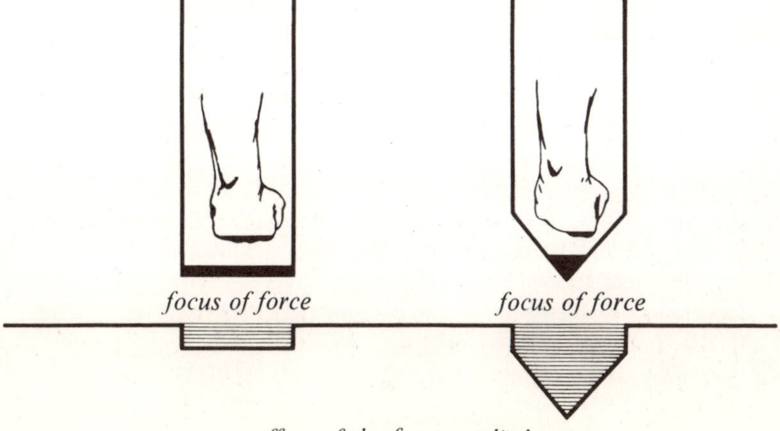

effect of the force applied

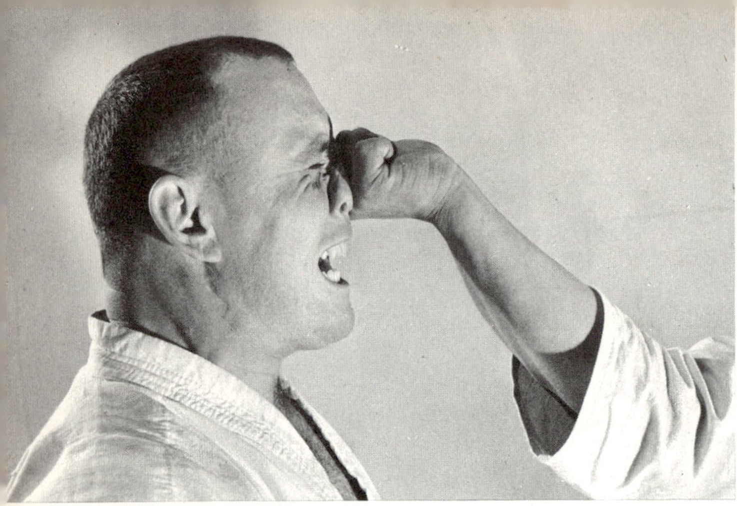

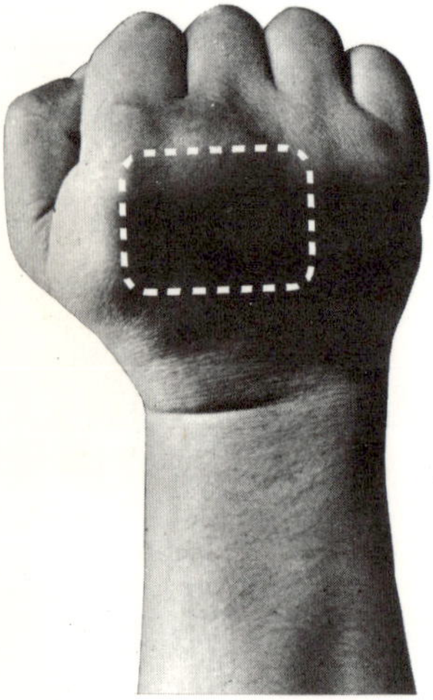

inverted fist ***(uraken)***

The fist is formed in the same way and the striking area is the same as that of the forefist, but when we use it we simply turn it upside down. The inverted fist is useful in an upward thrust that resembles an uppercut and in striking both to the right and left. When we practice inverted fist techniques we should be careful to train thoroughly in rotating the fist to the outside at the instant of contact. We also use the inverted fist in a large number of descending strikes.

knife hand ***(shuto)***

Put your thumb on top of your open hand, and turn the back of your hand either up, down, or out. This is the position you will use in what is commonly called the "karate chop," in attacks to the face, shoulder, or abdominal region. It is also effective as a block against thrusts, strikes, and kicks.

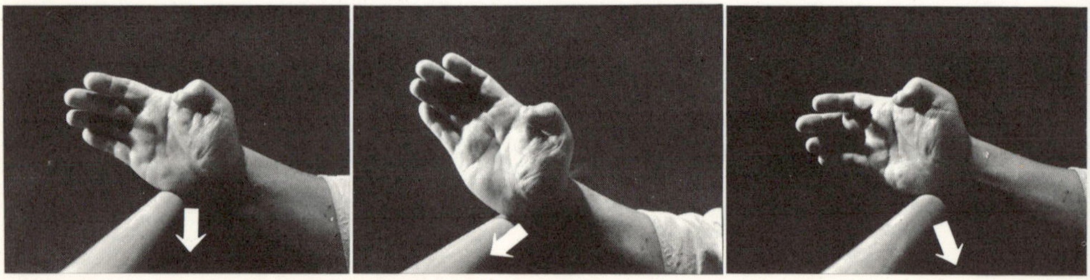

A B C

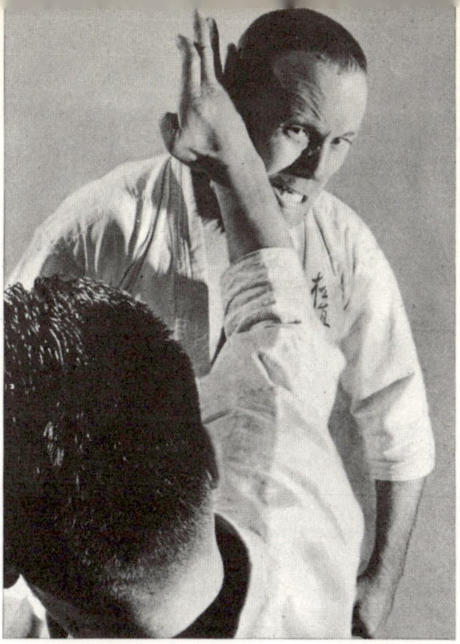

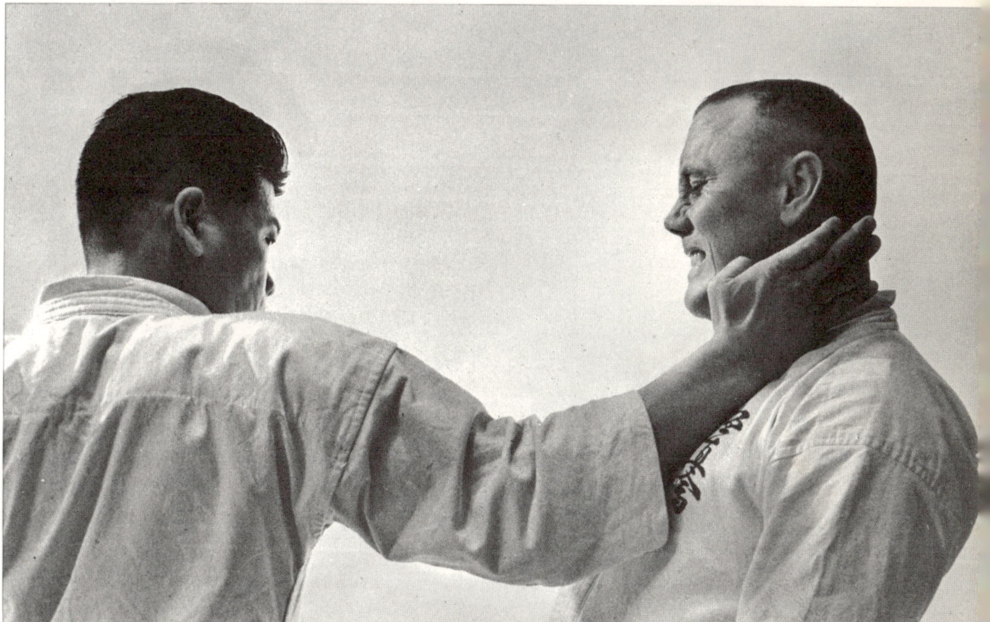

■ The first important way to use the knife hand is the descending strike from straight above, as you see it done in photograph A.
■ The second important method is to push the hand outward slightly at the moment of contact. (See B.)
■ The third method is to pull the hand slightly inward towards you at the moment of contact. (See C.)

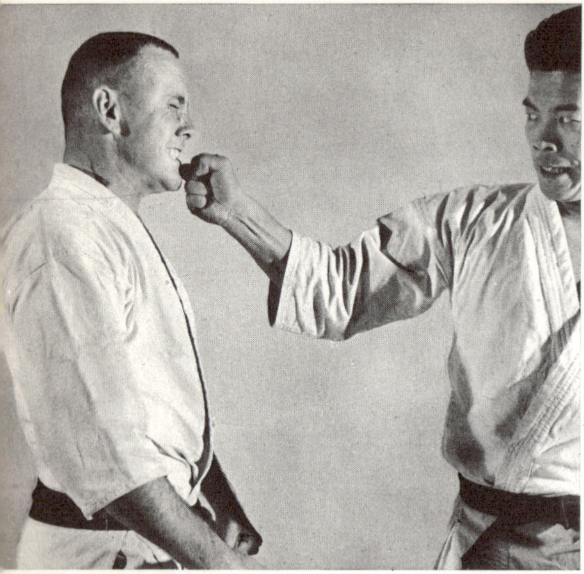

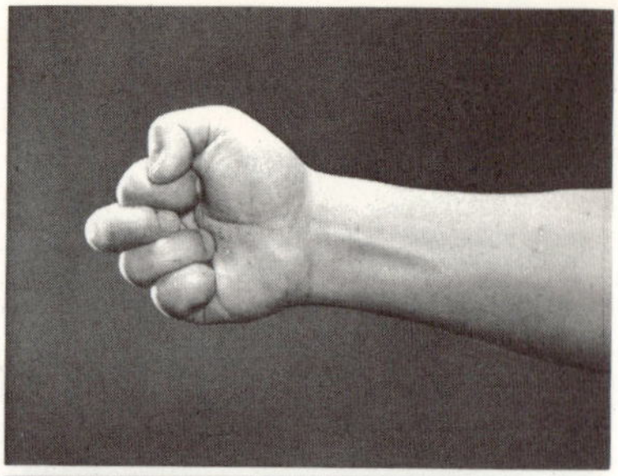

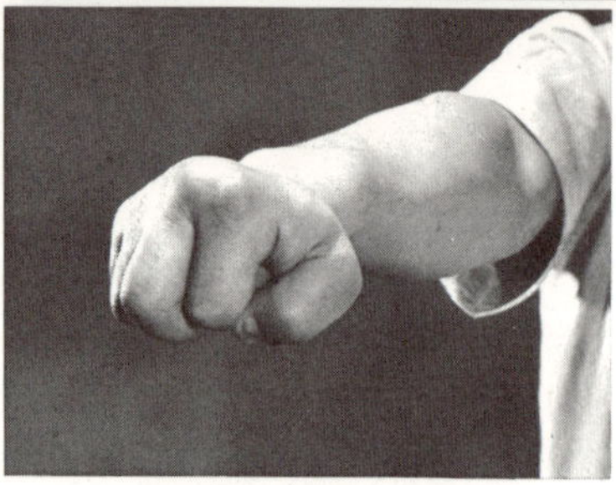

middle-finger one-knuckle fist

(nakayubi ipponken)

Jut only the second knuckle of your middle finger out. This position has the same uses as the forefinger one-knuckle fist.

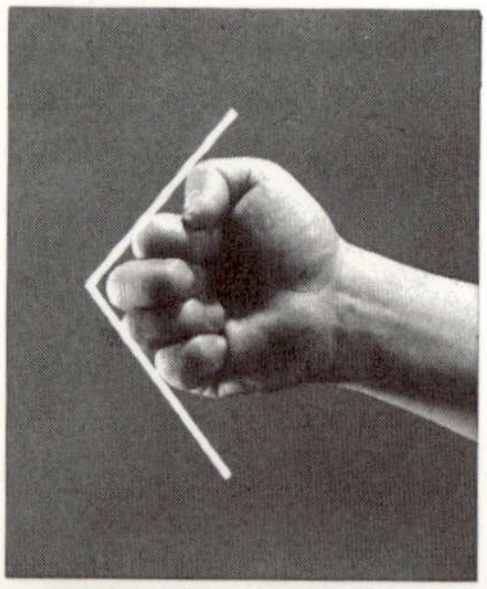

dragon's head fist *(ryutoken)*

Extend the knuckles of the forefinger, the middle finger, and the ring finger, with the middle finger higher than the others, as you see in the illustration. Uses are the same as in the forefinger one-knuckle fist.

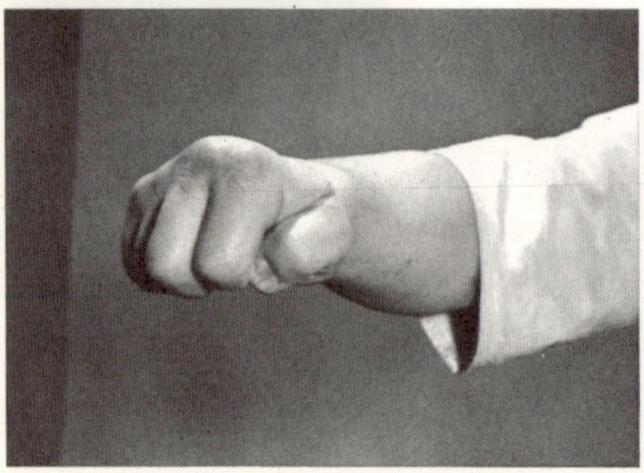

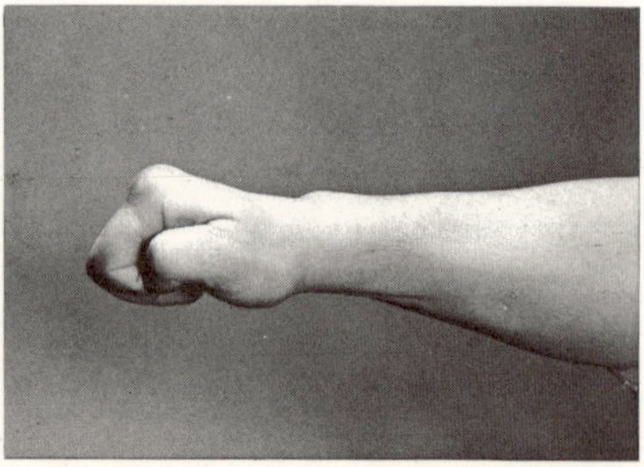

spear hand (bend-knuckle version)

Individual preferences account for many minor changes in the formation of this position. One of the strongest variations is the position with the fingers bent slightly at the first knuckle (see illustration). The uses are the same as those of the ordinary spear hand.

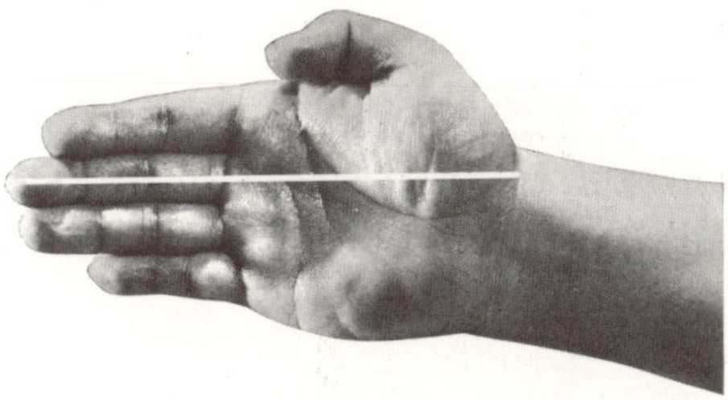

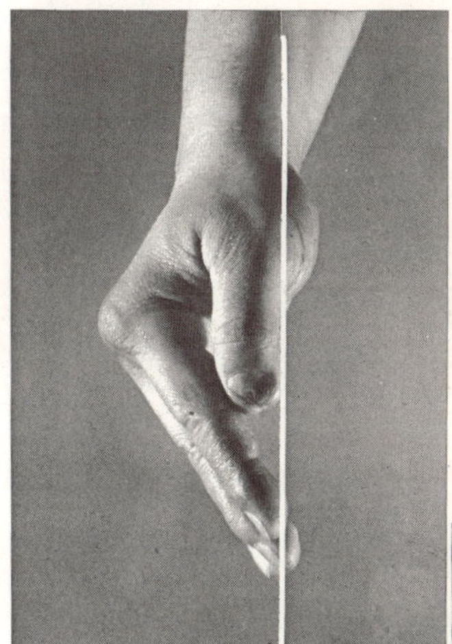

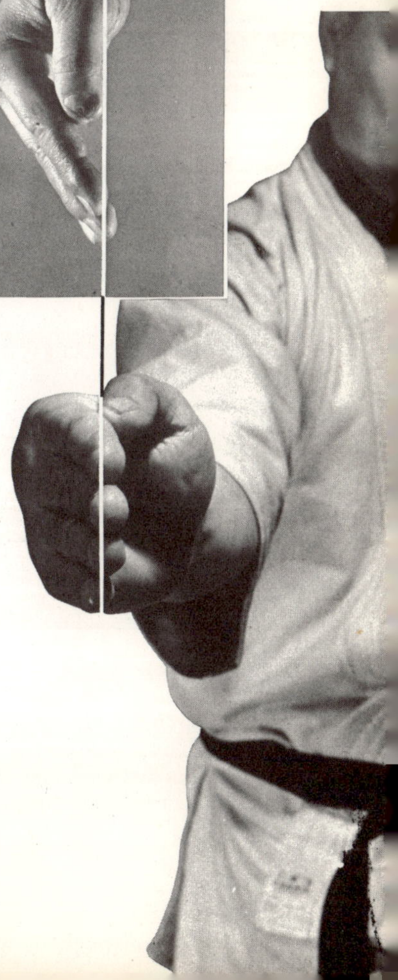

spear hand ***(nukite)***

Fingers are extended straight out, with thumb bent inward at the joint. This position is used in thrusts to the abdomenal area.

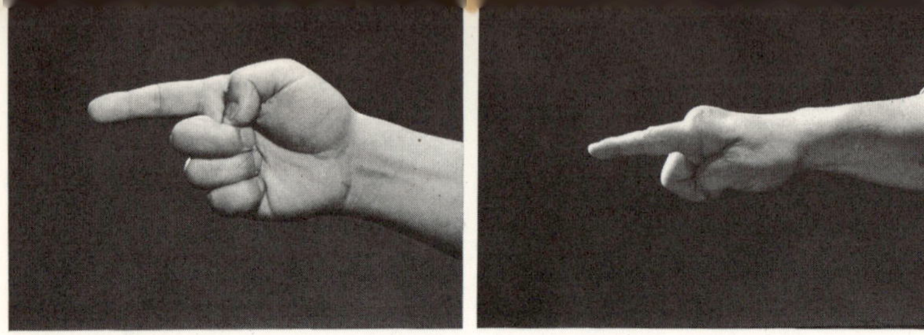

forefinger spear ***(ippon nukite)***

Turn the back of your hand up or out, depending on the use, and thrust with your extended forefinger.

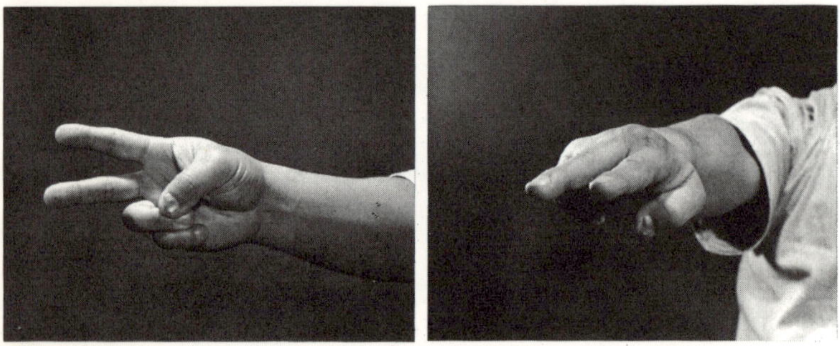

two-finger spear ***(nihon nukite)***

Fully extend the forefinger and the middle finger, and hold them in a V position. Uses same as in the forefinger one-knuckle fist.

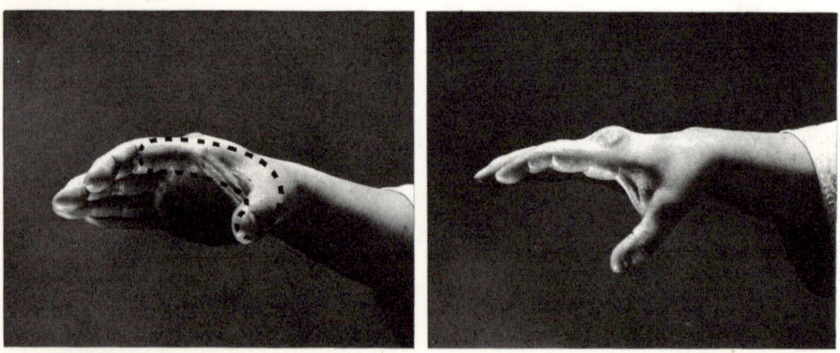

sword-peak hand ***(toho)***

Hold your hand out straight with the palm down and the thumb extended to the side. The striking point is the curved area between the thumb and the forefinger. Use this hand in scissors thrusts to the neck.

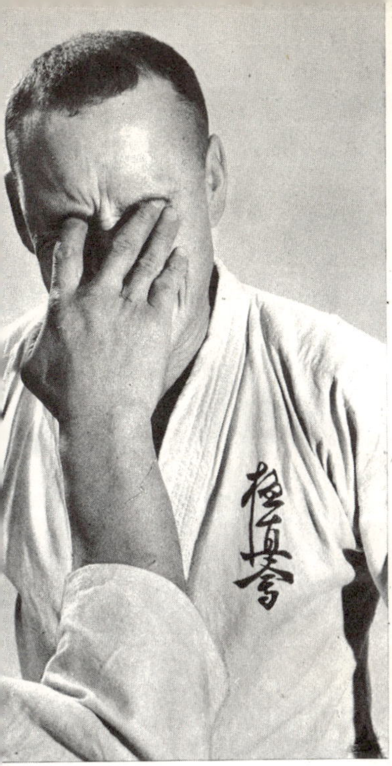

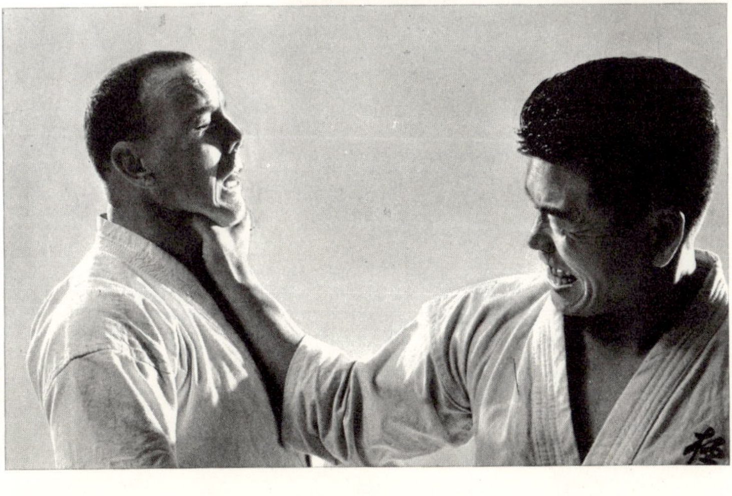

wrist ***(koken)***

This position too is very effective in both blocks and attacks though its attack applications are much more common in Chinese boxing (*kempo*) than in general karate. We can use it in descending strikes, rising strikes, inside strikes, and outside strikes. Because in this case we use the wrist where a number of the peripheral nerves come together, this position can cause injuries to your hand. Be sure that you keep the wrist well bent inward and that you put all the force in the striking zone. Though this position is not commonly used, we should not forget it because it can be most effective.

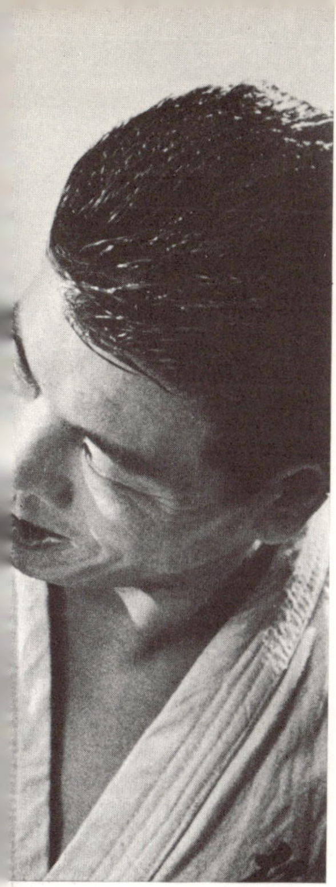

palm heel *(shotei)*

This hand position is useful in both attacks and blocks. It serves in both inside and outside blocks against kicks and thrusts and frequently in attacks to the stomach and to the face. When we use it in strikes it is essential to tense all five fingers.

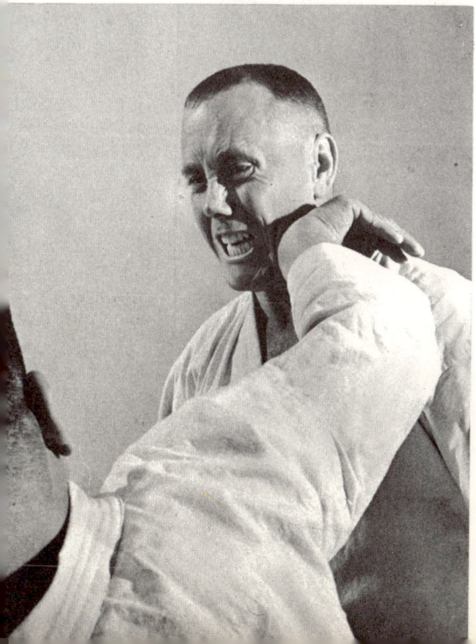

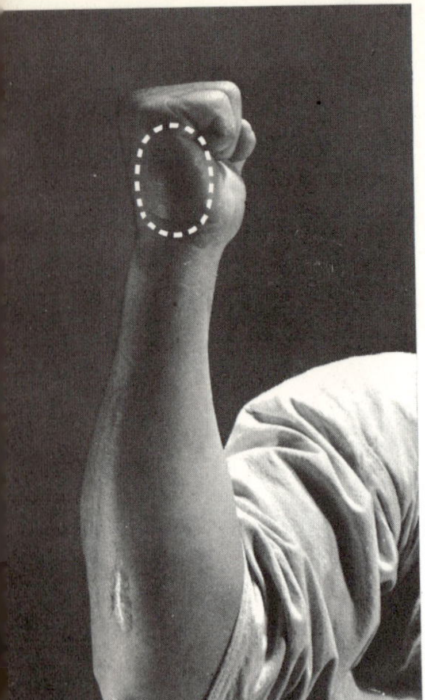

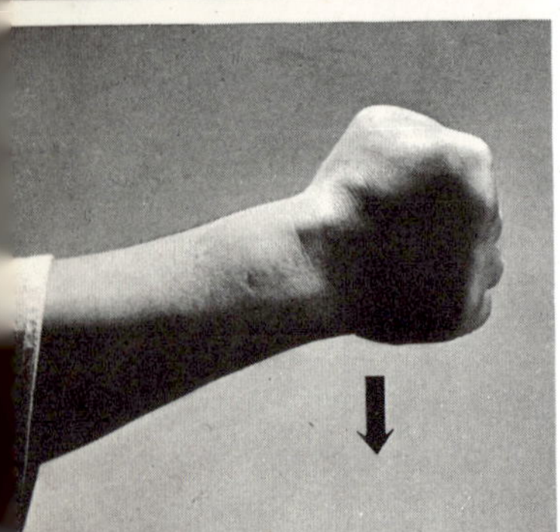

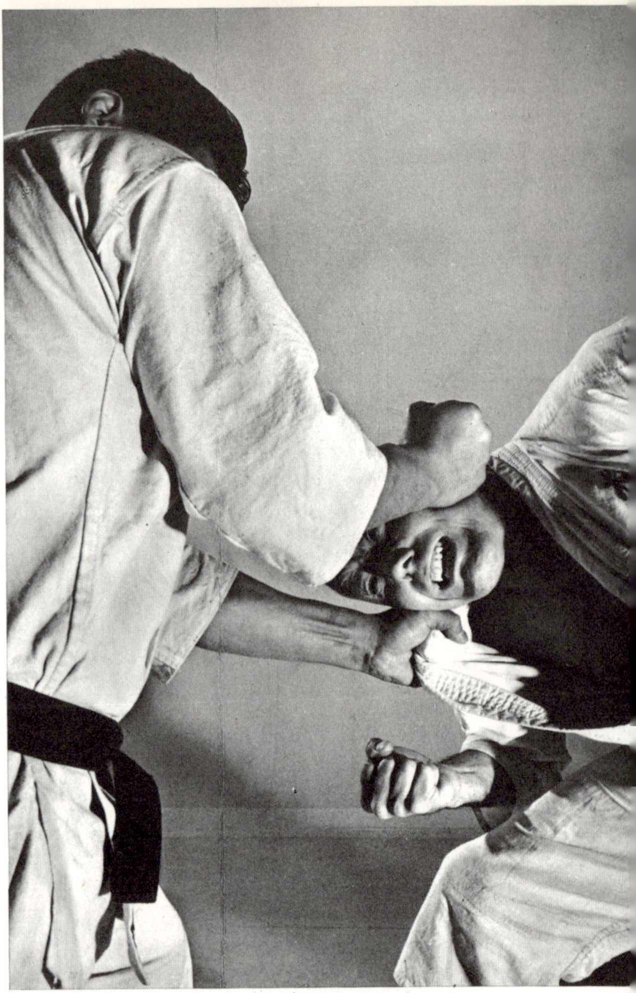

fist edge ***(tettsui)***

Though the fist is gripped in the same way as the forofist, the striking zone is the thick area at the base of the little-finger side of the hand. Since the striking zone is the same in this and in the knife hand, it is a good idea to practice the two together.

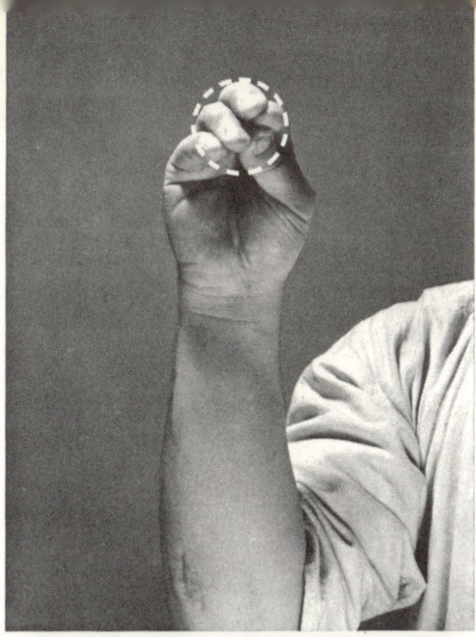

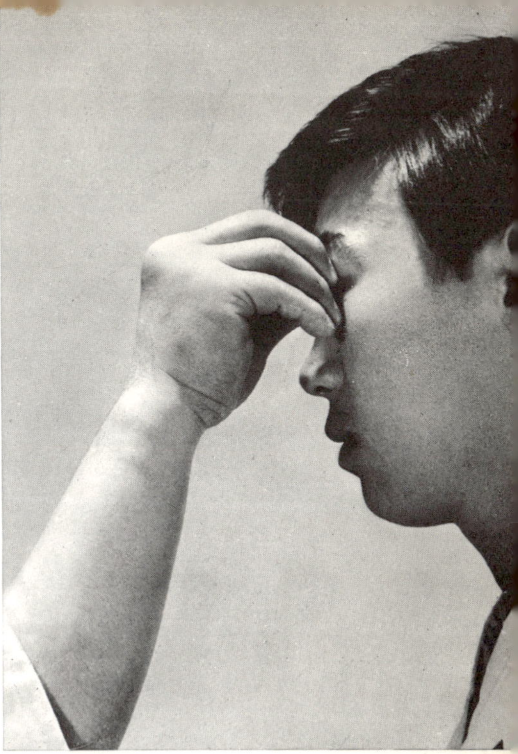

chicken-beak hand ***(keiko)***

Though more common in *kempo* than in karate, this is a strong position in which the fingers and thumb are pressed tightly together to form a point, and the back of the hand is turned up. The striking area is the point formed by the fingers. This hand is most effective in strikes straight ahead or on a horizontal line.

inner knife-hand ***(haito)***

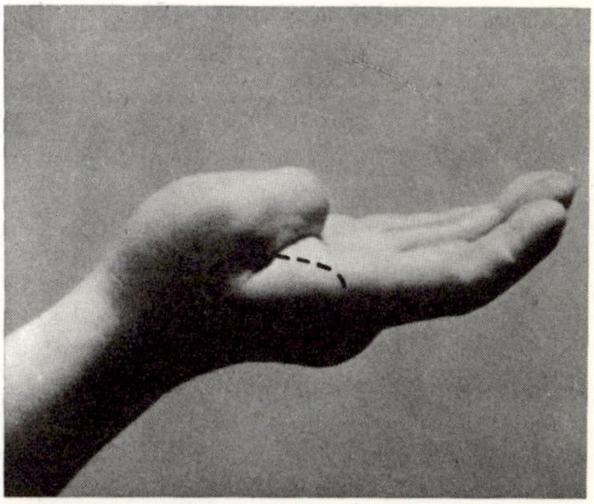

When properly done, the inner knife hand is actually easier to use than the knife hand, but it can be the cause of serious injury if you do not use it correctly. To form the inner knife hand we stretch our fingers straight out and bend the thumb under the hand tightly so that it stays in contact with the palm. Look closely at the photograph to learn the proper striking zone. This fist position is used both with the palm up and with the palm down.

half-clenched fist (*hiraken*)

Fold your thumb well in and the rest of your fingers at the second knuckle. Hold them all tightly into the palm. You strike to your opponent's face with the palm area, largely from the side, and to the ear area.

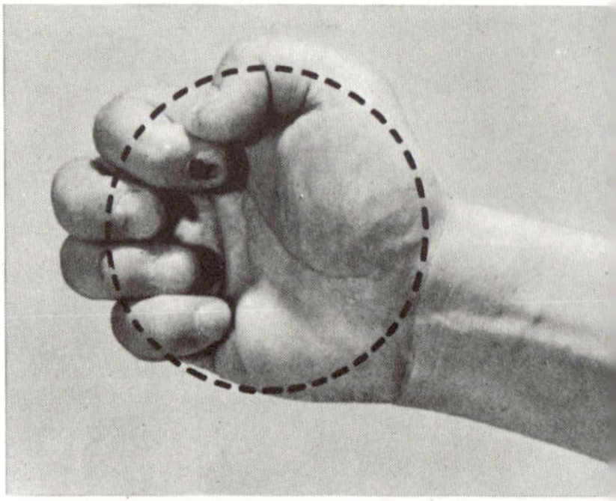

forearm (*kote*)

The hand is in the forefist position and the striking area is the lower section of the forearm. Because this is a difficult position to use, today there is probably only one master of it in the world. The three versions of this position depend on the striking area.

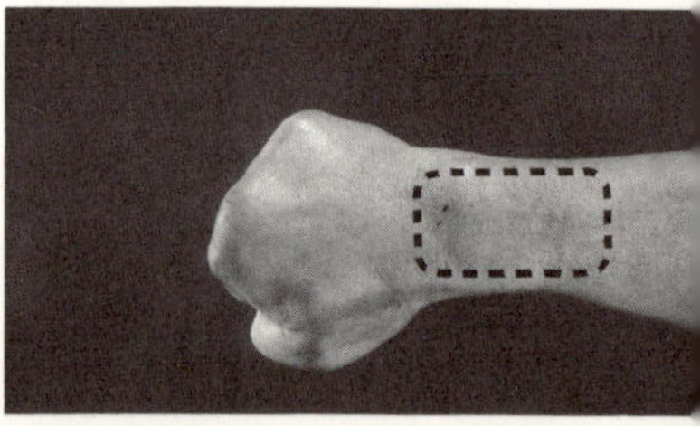

(A) *top forearm* (hira-kote)

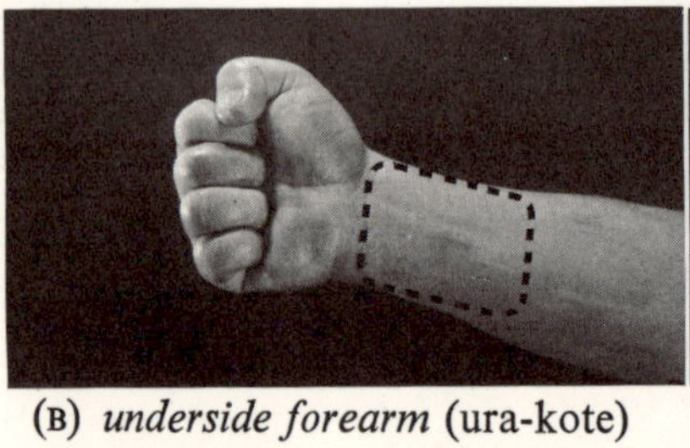

(B) *underside forearm* (ura-kote)

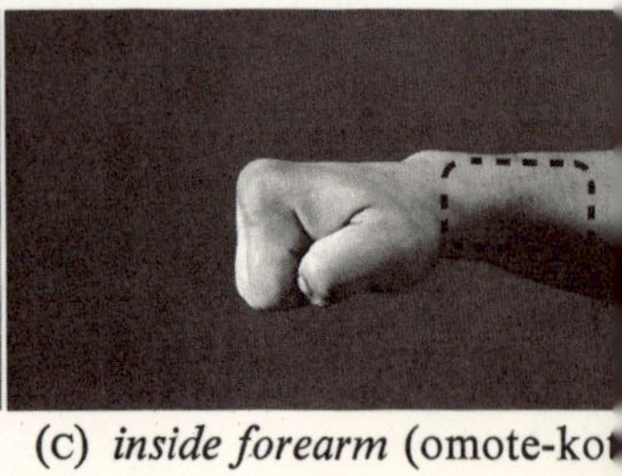

(C) *inside forearm* (omote-ko

thumb one-finger fist

(***oyayubi ipponken***)

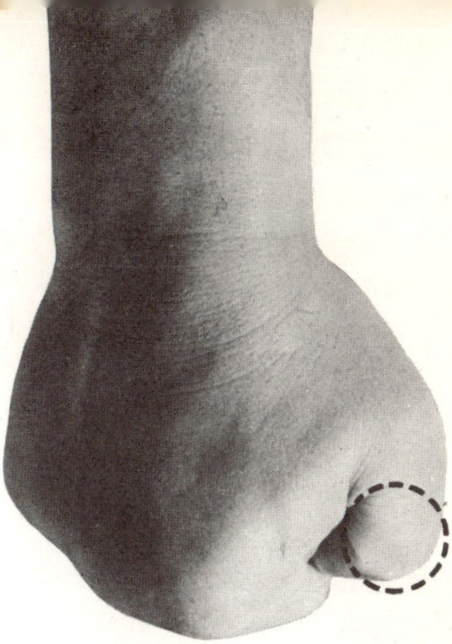

Here again we have a fist position that, though not in common use, is a highly advantageous one to know. It is formed as the forefist is, except that in this case we bend the thumb and press its tip hard down on the second knuckle of the forefinger. Because when used in strikes to the spot below the ear or to the temple this blow can cause instantaneous death, its use in such strikes is strictly forbidden in karate matches. Nonetheless, since the position can pack terrific power, it is good to learn it.

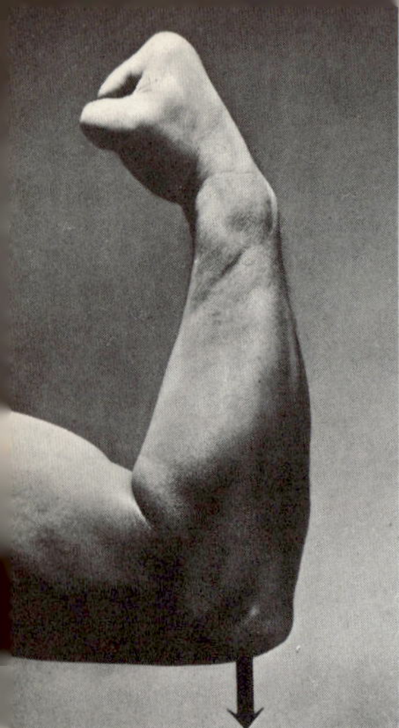

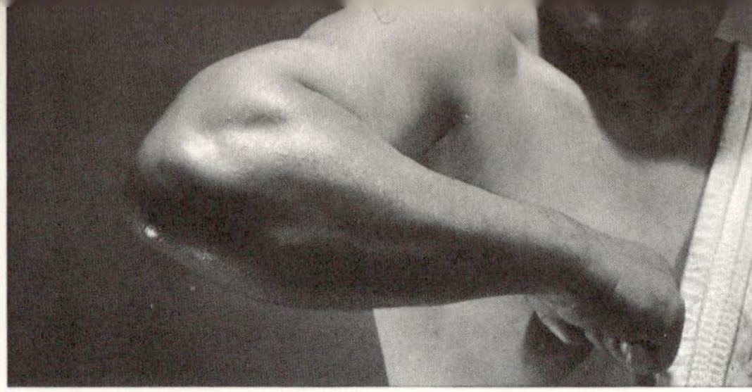

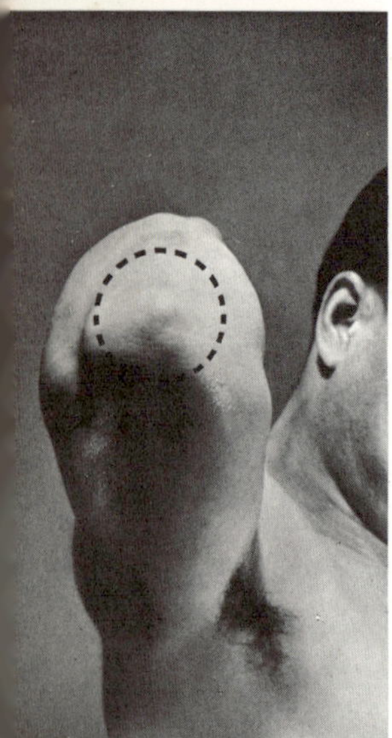

elbow ***(hiji)***

No other position gives as much power as this one, but because we strike with the elbow zone, the position's range is highly limited. It is, however, most effective when your opponent is at extremely close distance. The position is useful in upper, inside, outside, and descending strikes, and in elbow strikes to the chin, or stomach.

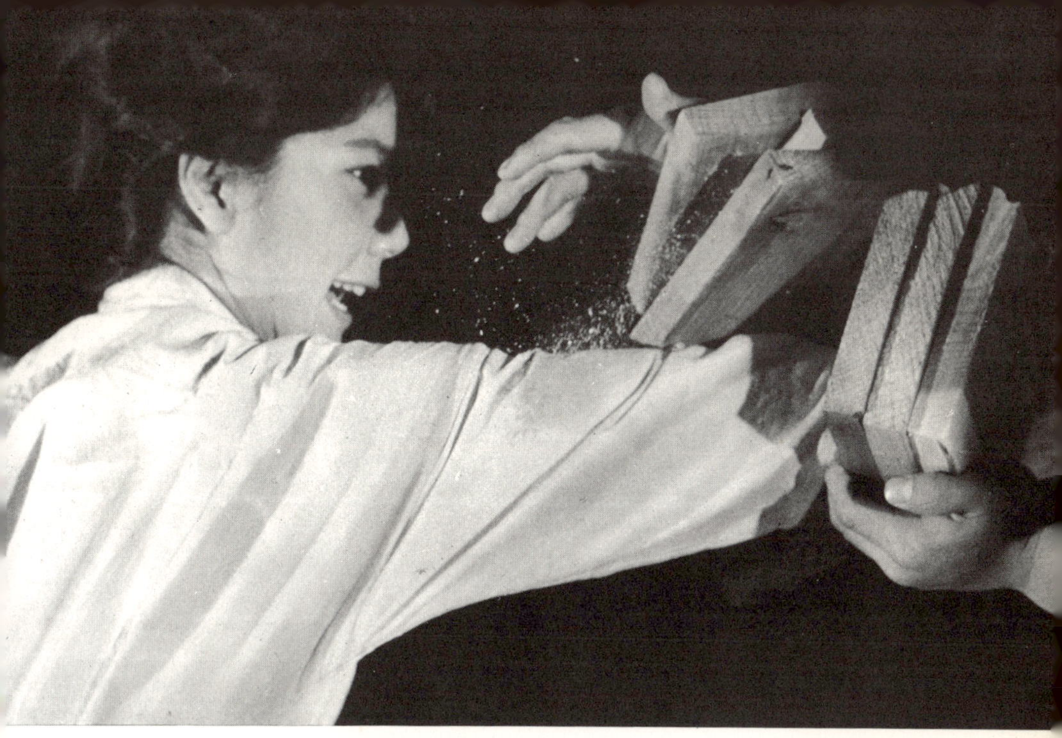

2. principle weapons : feet

Though the number of karate weapons formed with the feet is smaller than those formed with the hands and though we are not as likely to hurt or injure our feet as readily because the skin and flesh on them tends to be tougher, do not forget that, just as in the case of the hand strikes, in foot strikes too you need the cooperation of the ankle, the knee, and the thigh to generate the terrific force you want. This is particularly true in the case of the ankle snap. In all of the foot techniques and kicks a strong ankle and an effective ankle snap are most important.

knife foot ***(sokuto)***

The knife foot, generally used in side kicks, has an effect similar to that of the knife hand.

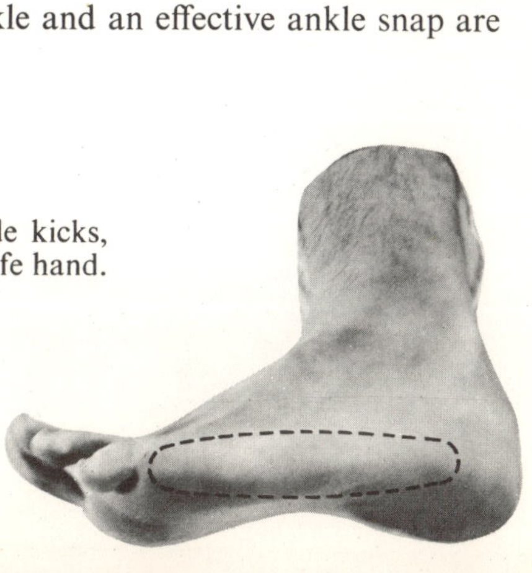

ball of the foot ***(chusoku)***

This position is effective in front kicks to the opponent's stomach or in roundhouse kicks to the chin or ribs.

When you use the ball of the foot, be sure to keep your toes bent back as far as possible because doing so strengthens the contact zone. Kicks with the ball of the foot demand a powerful spring action in your knee. The ball of the foot is similar in effect to the forefist.

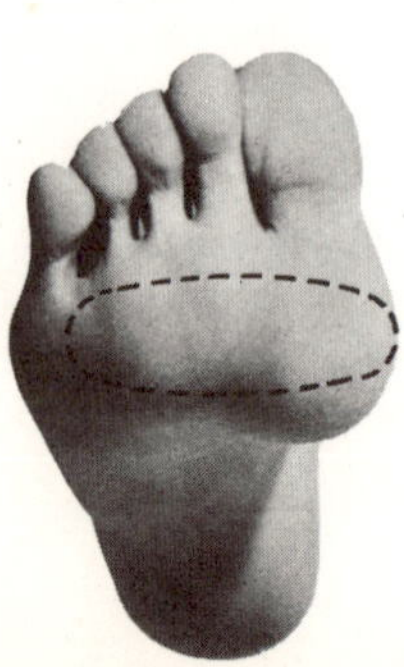

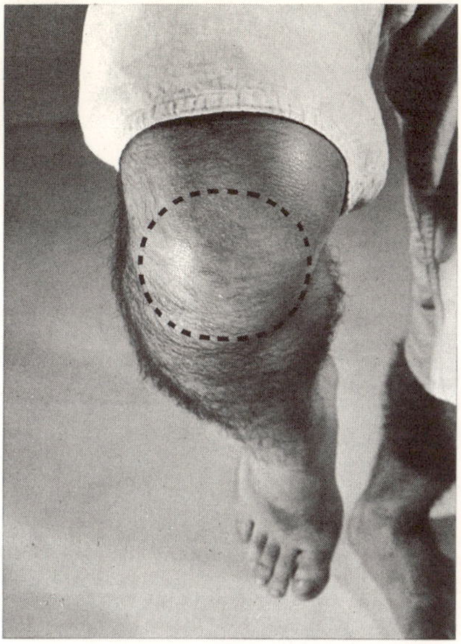

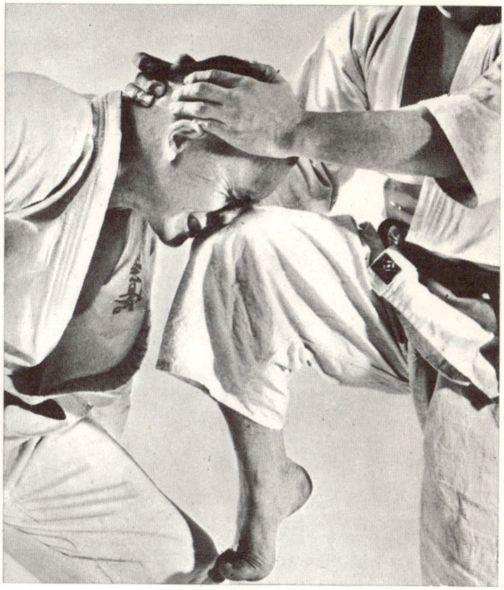

knee ***(hiza)***

We use the knee to attack to the groin, face, or ribs of an opponent who has grabbed us. We also sometimes pull our opponent's head downward and strike it with our knees.

The muscle that supplies the main force for the knee kicks is in the thigh. To use your knee effectively you must have strong hips. When you kick with the knee, be sure to keep your toes pointed downward. The knee is similar in effect to the elbow.

arch ***(teisoku)***

Used in kicking to the arms or to the abdomen.

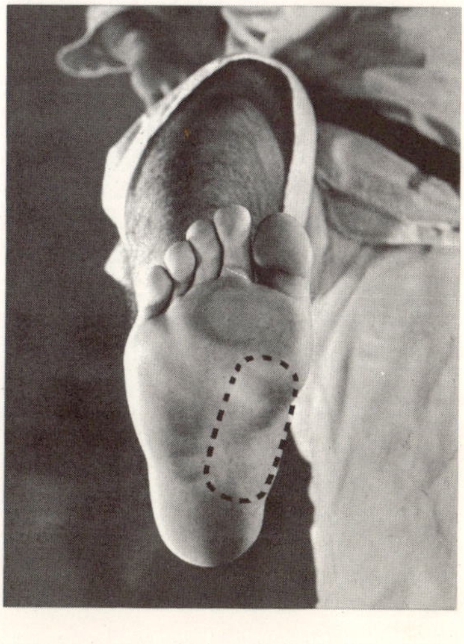

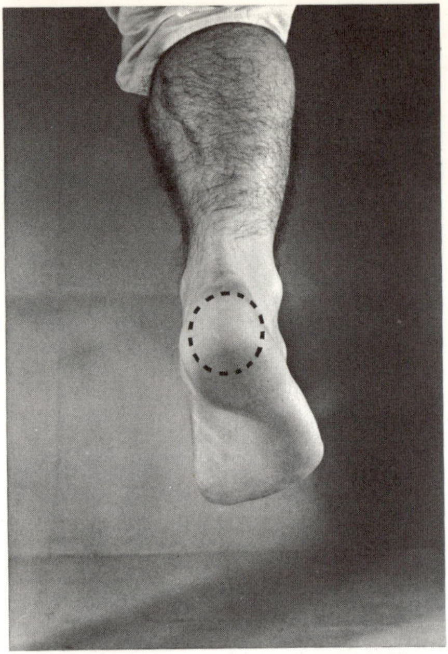

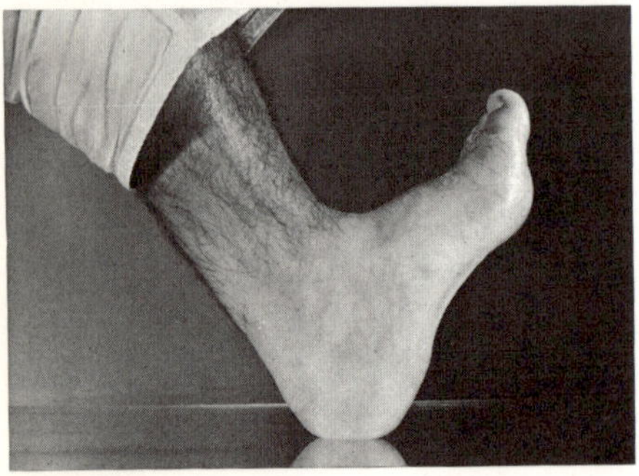

heel ***(kakato)***

The heel is effective in turns and backward kicks to your opponent's abdomen or face. It is also a good weapon to use in the final blow when your opponent is down, or as a means of striking back when you yourself are down.

instep ***(haisoku)***

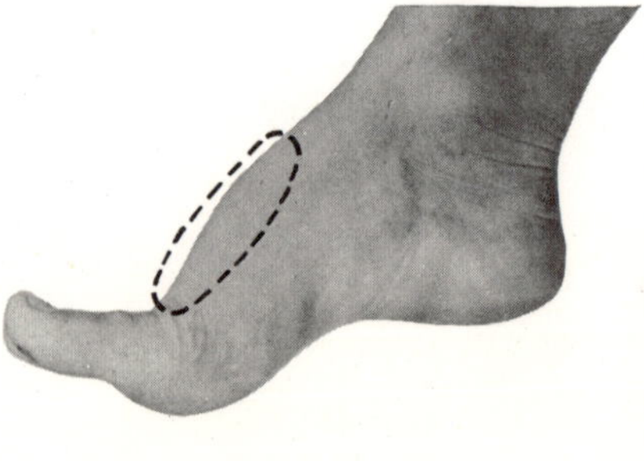

We use the instep in kicking to our opponent's groin or in kicking to his stomach, face, ears, or ribs as we turn our own bodies.

When you use the instep, be sure to add a snap to your movements. The snap requires that your ankle be strong. Remember to keep all of your toes together and to tense them at the moment of contact. You can think of this weapon as similar to the inverted fist.

3. head

Though the head thrusts occur infrequently in karate, they are of great interest as they turn up often in North China, Korea, Mongolia, and Russia. Though too much use of these head techniques is not good for the body, they are effective in close-range fighting, because the comparatively heavy head, can generate unbelievable concentrations of power.

head thrusts

Because of their great effect, head thrusts are frequently most useful when the chips seem to be down.

In general, we can divide head thrusts into two categories:

Head-on thrusts

Left or right thrusts

Two other thrusts of interest are the back

thrust for use when an opponent has seized us from behind and the upward thrust for use as we rise from a seated position to a standing one.

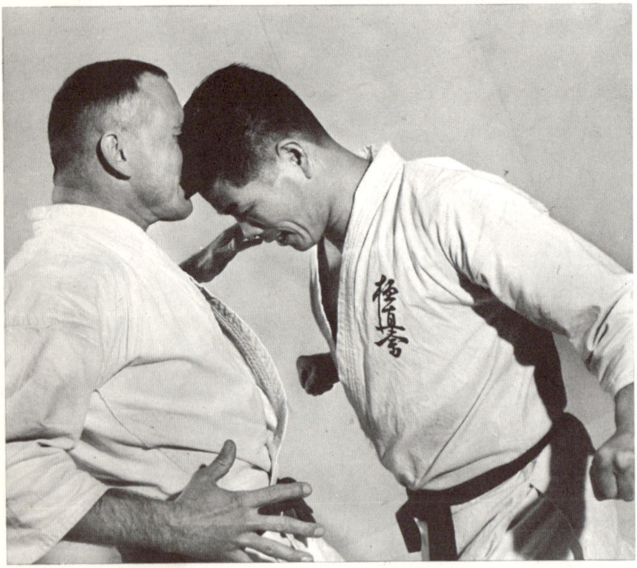

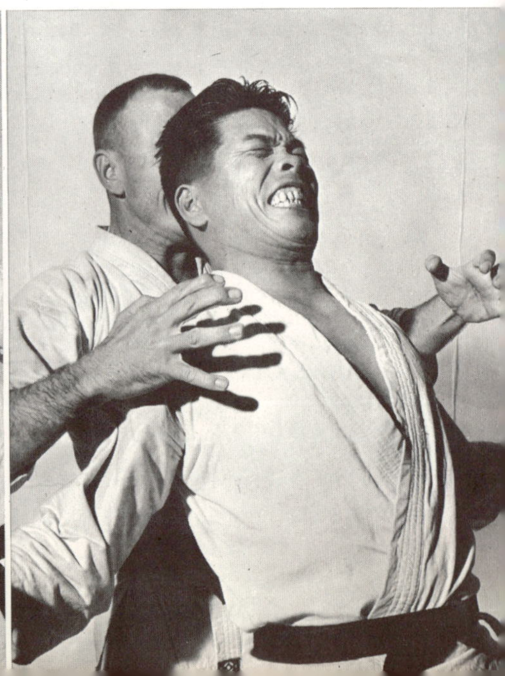

CHAPTER

2 preparatory calisthenics

The distinctive feature of karate preparatory calisthenics is that they are all aimed at strengthening or limbering the joints, rather than the muscles. All of the calisthenics on these pages involve the use of the finger or toe joints, the ankles, the knees, the vertebrae, the wrists, the elbows, or the neck.

Though by no means as entertaining as actual karate practice, calisthenics are necessary. Without sufficient preparatory exercise, the karate player is apt to find himself getting dizzy or stiff in actual combat practice and may even end up with pulled muscles. It is essential to follow a basic calisthenics routine daily to stay fit.

ankle exercise (I)

Lift the right foot and turn the ankle around in a circle a number of times. Repeat with the left foot.

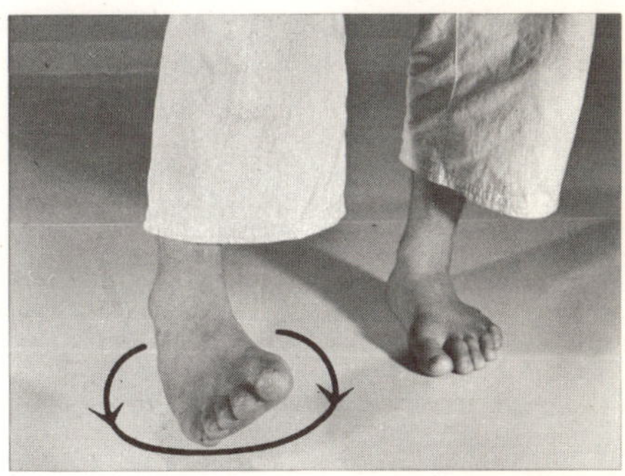

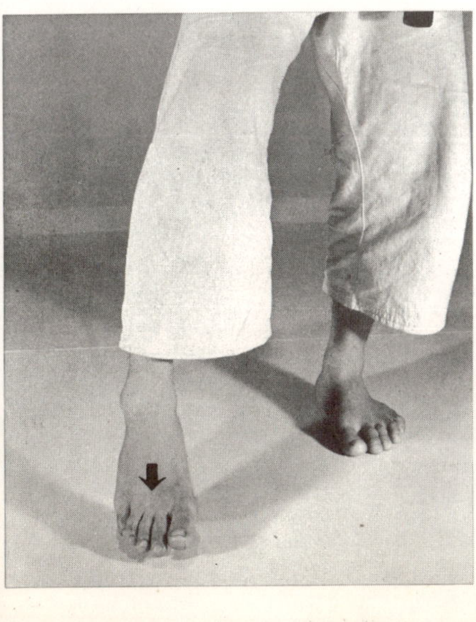

ankle exercise (II)

Tense the toes and thrust them forward lightly.

achilles tendon exercise

Crouch on toes with heels raised. Rock back onto the heels, straightening the legs and raising the toes.

leg-spreading exercise

The object is to spread the legs out as straight as possible. Though this is difficult to do at first, it is vital to the development of a strong kick. Be careful not to strain in the first attempts. Work up to a 180° leg spread gradually, but remember that a good kick demands mastery of this position. When you have spread your legs, bend your body toward the left foot, and grasp the left ankle with both hands. Touch your forehead to your left knee, return to the original position, and repeat the exercise in the opposite direction.

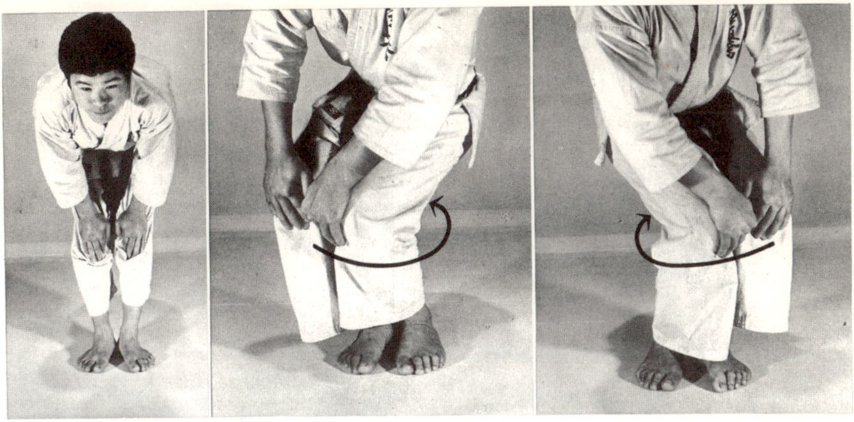

knee exercise

Crouch in a deep knee-bend position, and move the knees around in a circle. When the circle is complete, reverse the direction and repeat.

hip exercise (I)

Stand with legs spread wide apart and hands clasped behind your head. Bend over forward and then backward. As you repeat the exercise, gradually bring your feet closer together, ending the exercise in a closed-foot position. Bringing the legs together is an essential part of this exercise.

hip exercise (II)

Start from a normal stance, keeping the legs straight, bend forward and place your palms flat on the floor in front of your feet. Lift hands, turn them around, and place palms down flat behind the feet. Resume the original stance and repeat.

thigh joint exercise

Holding the ankle as straight as possible, put the sole of the foot flat on the floor. Raise the sole, and turn the toes upward, at the same time lowering the body so that the leg is as nearly flat on the ground as possible. Hold the knee straight with the hand. Repeat this exercise with the other leg.

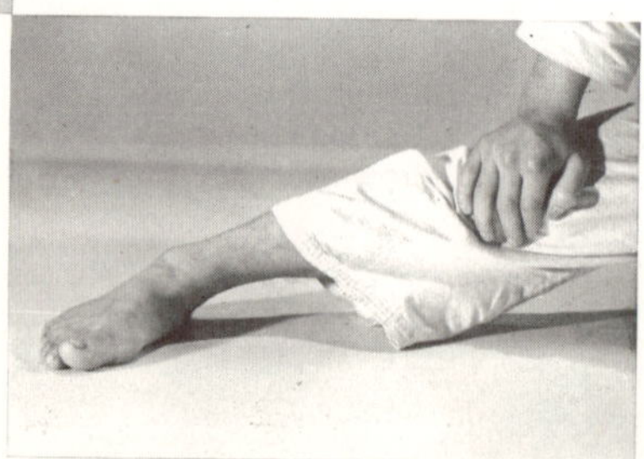

forward bend exercise

Spread legs out straight, and grasp shins. Holding shins, bend your body forward until your forehead touches the ground.

forward bend exercise with feet together

This is variant on the previous exercise. Sit with your thighs spread outward but with the soles of the feet together. Bend over until your forehead touches your feet. This is a good exercise for the back and the hip joints.

toe joint exercise

Assume a parallel stance, holding the sash with the hands. In alternation, raise first the big toes and then the other toes, rocking the weight from side to side on the soles of the feet.

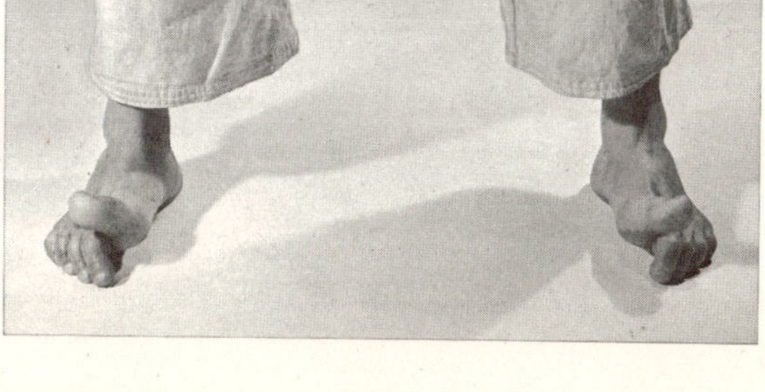

push-ups with legs spread

Assume the position for a push-up, but with legs spread outward as far as possible. Lower and raise your body with your arms, as in ordinary push-ups. This is a good exercise for the shoulders and arms.

hip and back exercise

Stand with legs apart, and bend over at the waist, holding the legs straight. Bend so as to touch your left foot with your right hand, at the same time raising your left arm behind your back. Swing your arms around and touch your right foot with your left hand. Continue swinging back and forth, not returning to standing position until the exercise has ended. Swing both arms with force.

neck exercise

Stand naturally with legs apart about shoulder width. Bend the neck forward, then backward as far as possible. Returning to the original position, turn your head as far as possible to the left, then to the right. Returning to the original position, turn your head in a circle to the left, then to the right.

arm exercise with clasped hands

Assume a *sanchin* stance (see Chapter Five), with arms bent upward and palms inward, put palms together before sash. Bring your arms upward, with palms together. When your arms are in front of chest, pull them inward, still keeping the palms together. Turning your fingers upward, bring the arms down as far as possible. This exercise is good for the muscles of the underside of the arms.

variations on the push-up

The push-up is a very effective body-building exercise. For karate purposes, it is best to do push-ups with the hand held in a fist rather than flat. Only the knuckles of the forefinger and the middle finger should touch the floor. Push-ups in which you raise the body with the fingers rather than with the fist or palm greatly strengthen the grasp. They are particularly valuable to those wishing to try their hand at breaking tiles, bricks, or other such objects.

three-finger push-up

(thumb, forefinger, and middle finger)

two-finger push-up

(thumb and forefinger)

CHAPTER **3**

stances

Standing and walking are two of the most important things in human life. Proper walking, the more difficult of these two, depends on proper standing. In turn, in karate, without mastery of stance, walking, kicking and the forms are impossible to perform.

Karate includes a wide variety of stances, each devised to suit the needs of given techniques, and most derived from and classified in Chinese *kempo*. The twelve most vital stances we have included demand complete mastery.

normal stance *(heisoku-dachi)*

Feet together and parallel pointing straight ahead, stand straight.

In the following four stances the upper body remains in the position it is in for the normal stance. Only the positions of the feet change.

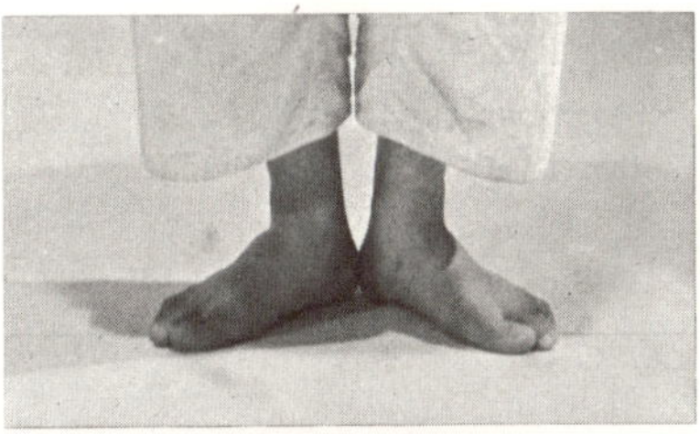

open-toes stance *(musubi-dachi)*

Tips of the toes pointed out, heels together; stand straight.

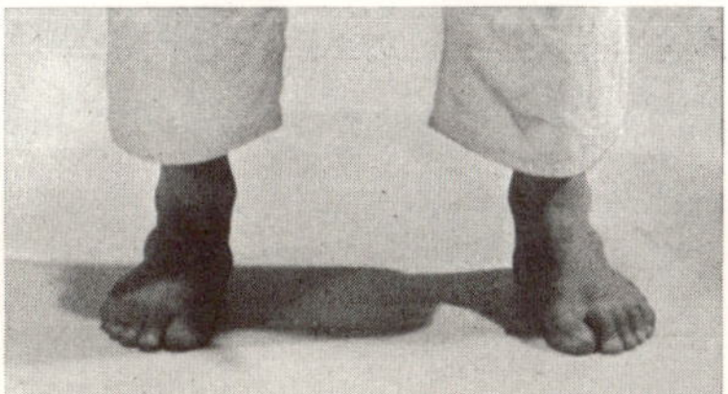

parallel open stance *(heiko-dachi)*

Legs apart about the width of your shoulders with feet parallel and pointed straight ahead.

forward leaning stance
(zenkutsu-dachi)

Put one foot forward, bend the knee of the forward leg. Lean your body forward, and keep your back leg straight. The forward foot points straight ahead, and the rear foot points slightly to the outside.

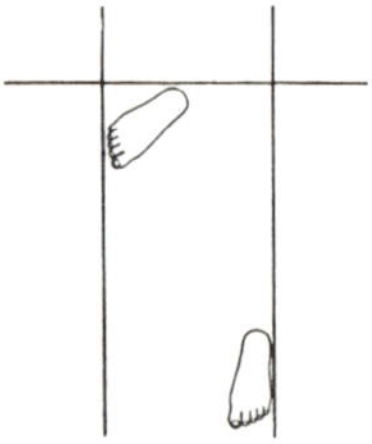

back leaning stance
(kokutsu-dachi)

Put one foot forward, tense the toes of that foot, and lean your torso back. The toes of the forward foot are pointed straight ahead. Distribute your body weight 70% on the back leg and 30% on the forward one.

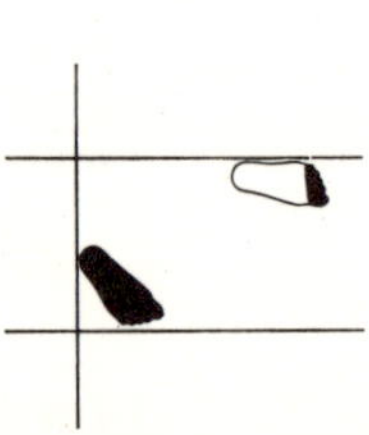

sanchin **stance** ***(sanchin-dachi)***

This, one of the most frequently used stances, has two versions, the right and the left *sanchin* stances. In the right stance, put your left foot forward, draw your right foot slightly back, and point the toes of both feet slightly inward. The foot position you see in the chart is for a left *sanchin* stance; the right foot is forward.

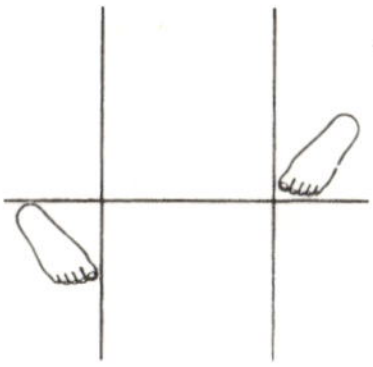

straddle stance ***(kiba-dachi)***

Squat into a position similar to one you might use on horseback. Toes are pointed forward and feet are parallel.

cat stance *(nekoashi-dachi)*

The foot position in this stance is similar to the shape of a cat's rear feet. Put one foot forward, bend the instep of that foot so that the heel is off the ground. Distribute your body weight 90% on the back leg so that the front foot is always ready for a kick.

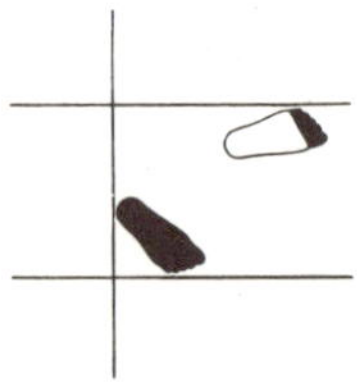

sumo stance *(shiko-dachi)*

Feet spread about twice shoulder width and toes pointed out, straighten your legs first, then half squat. The Japanese name of this stance, *shiko-dachi*, derives from the name of a famous stance Japanese sumo wrestlers use.

hooked stance ***(kake-dachi)***

Hook your left foot behind your right foot. Put most of your body weight on your right leg. Turn the toes of only your left foot in.

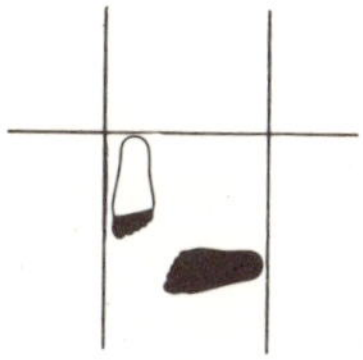

crane stance
(tsuruashi-dachi)

The name derives from the position's similarity to the way a crane stands on one leg. Put one foot lightly on one knee so that all of your weight is on the one foot.

CHAPTER

4 thrusts

NOW THAT WE HAVE EXPLAINED the preparatory calisthenics and stances we will move on to basic techniques training. Basic techniques are essential, particularly for a beginner. Repeat one exercise on an average of more than thirty times each session, and a session of all the basic techniques will require from 40 to 50 minutes. As we have already explained, the *sanchin* stance is the best for exercising. The open stance and the straddle stance are unsuitable.

The *sanchin* stance is also good practice for concentrating your strength in the pit of your stomach. As we said earlier, in this stance tense only the abdomen, the dorsal muscles, and the striking areas.

Never neglect practicing the basic techniques, though there are some people who do, because these techniques are the building blocks from which we construct the karate formal exercises.

The life of karate is practice fighting, or *kumite*, and the life of the *kumite*, in turn, is the basic techniques. Because these techniques are the mother's womb of karate formal exercises, it is important to practice them more often than anything else. Though there are a number of special techniques for people who have mastered the basics and want to develop the high technical level that karate demands, advanced techniques do not appear in the present work.

The following photographs and explanations will demonstrate both the correct and the incorrect methods of performing basic techniques training.

a. correct thrust

The method of thrusting in the middle thrust from the *sanchin* stance is very important. The places to tense in thrusts are the abdomen, the dorsal muscles, and the striking areas. The people who hold that any thrusting method is all right do not understand the essence of karate and are making a great error. Because the thrust is the heart of karate, if your thrust is incorrect, your karate will be also.

The following photographs illustrate thrusting methods in both head-on and top views.

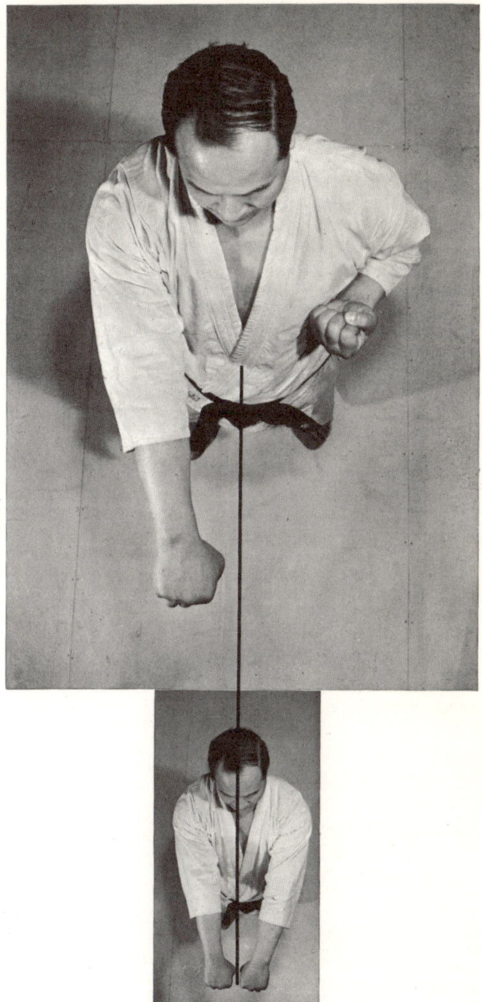

Thrust with both hands stretched forward at the angle at which they would be if your open hands met.

The following photographs illustrate why it is not good to thrust too far to the inside or the outside.

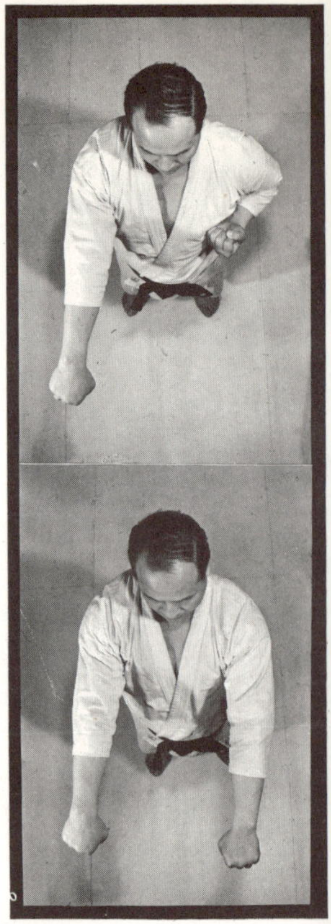

INCORRECT THRUST

In this thrust the hands are separated the distance of the width of the shoulders.

As you see in the photograph, if the thrust is too far to the outside, your opponent can catch you with a reverse and swing you to the inside.

Again, as you see in the photograph, if the thrust is too far to the inside, your opponent can block it with either the palm heel or with a knife hand.

In conclusion, I think the reader can understand the importance of correct thrusting. Of course, only a person who has practiced karate for many years will be able to block a thrust easily.

forefist middle thrust

(seiken chudan-tsuki)

1. Turn the back of your withdrawn hand down and bring it to your chest, (see photograph).
2. Your fist should be facing as it would be if you stretched both hands straight out in front of you and joined your fingers. Your fist should be at about the height of your own stomach.
3. In the course of the thrust, twist your arm so that the back of the thrusting hand is up.
4. Put all your strength into your fist at the instant of contact.
5. Bring your hand to a quick halt at the spot at which it makes contact.
6. At first, your withdrawn hand should be in the beginning position, but during the thrust it should turn so that the top of the hand faces down. Draw this hand in as close to the body as possible for speed and strength in the thrusting fist.
7. Relax your shoulders, put the shoulder of the thrusting arm slightly forward, and hold your body so that it does not twist. Tense the big toes and the solar plexus. If the solar plexus is stable, so will the upper half of the body be. Keep your hips balanced.
8. Tuck your chin in, and always keep your line of sight directed straight at where an opponent's face would be, even though there may be no opponent.
9. Practice at first with one hand at a time, right, then left, then right, then left. Gradually, as you make progress, you will practice with series of right-left, then on to the three-phase practice of right-left-right in a continuous series. Pay particularly close attention to mastering points 4, 6, 7, and 8 in the thrusts and strikes, because these are basic technical moves that are almost the same in many other techniques.

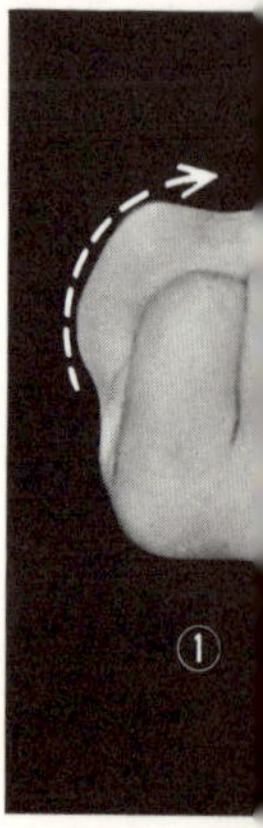

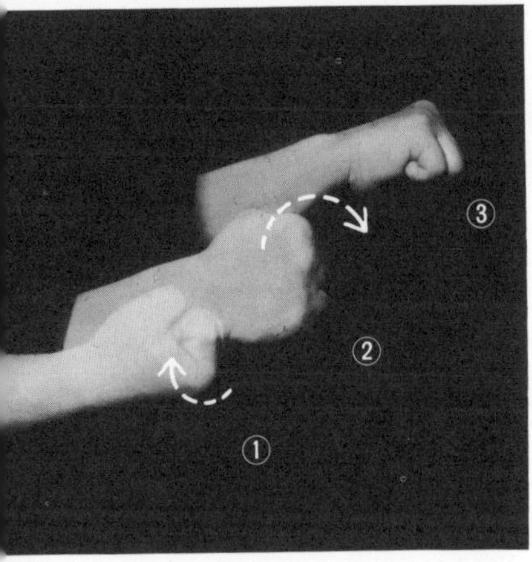

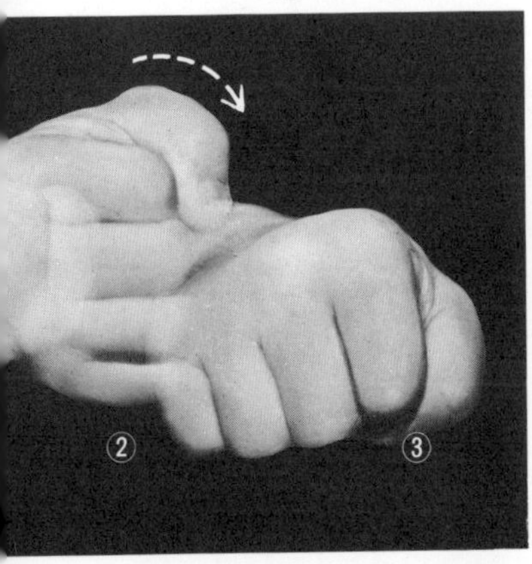

It is more effective not to extend your arm fully, as you see in the photograph, when you perform a forefist thrust. Bending your arm more than the model in the photograph reduces your thrust's effect.

forefist strike to the chin
(seiken ago-uchi)

Hold the withdrawn hand with the back facing upward and with the hand slightly away from the chest. This thrust differs from the middle and upper thrusts in that you instantaneously bring the thrusting hand back straight to your body after the thrust. You do not halt your hand after it has made contact.

forefist roundhouse strike (or thrust)
(seiken mawashi-uchi)

Begin with your fist in the small of your back, and swing your hand outward and bend your elbow. With a roundhouse movement strike the opponent on the side of the head. Bring your fist to a halt at the instant of contact.

front inverted-fist strike

(uraken shomen-uchi)

Invert both fists, and keep both elbows close to the front of your chest. Leaving your fist inverted, strike at your opponent's face. Snap the striking fist back to its original position at the instant of contact. Of course, all movements must be fast.

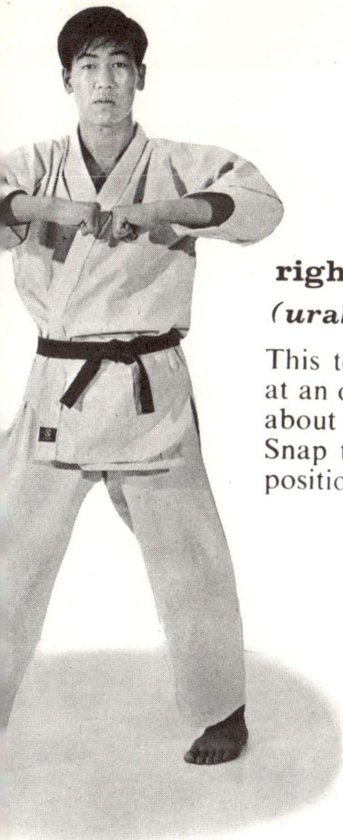

right-left inverted-fist strike

(uraken sayu-uchi)

This technique is used for striking sideways at an opponent. Your fists should be back at about nipple height in the center of your chest. Snap the striking hand back to its original position immediately after impact.

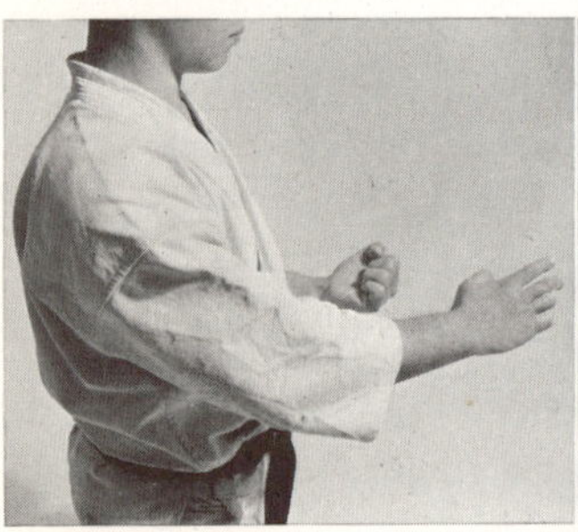

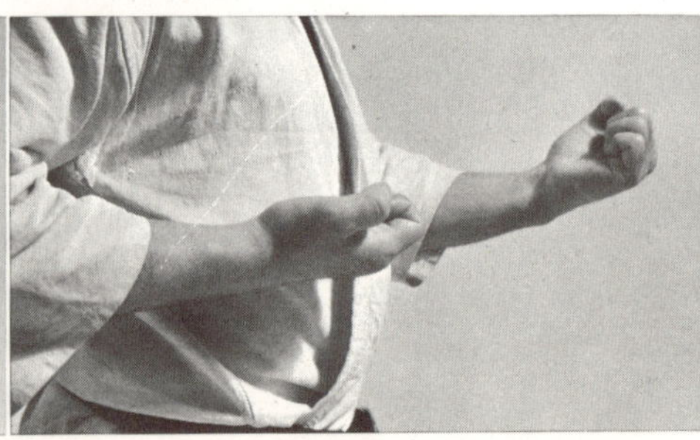

inverted-fist low thrust

(uraken shita-uchi)

Squat slightly in a straddle stance. Bring your fist to a halt at the moment of contact. Snap your wrist slightly as it makes contact.

inverted-fist strike to the spleen
(uraken hizo-uchi)

This technique is used to strike sideways to your opponent's spleen. At the moment of contact twist your hand slightly to the outside, then snap it back to your body immediately.

knife-hand strike to the collarbone
(shuto sakotsu-uchi)

This strike swings down from above to your opponent's collarbone. At the moment of contact pull your withdrawn hand in tight, and twist your hips slightly to concentrate all your strength in the striking hand.

knife-hand strike to the face
(shuto gammen-uchi)

The striking hand travels in a circle from the area behind your ear to the opponent's temple. Without letting your hand swing outward, strike clean and direct. Halt the striking hand on contact, and when you strike with your other hand join the two, and bring them back together. Tense your abdomen firmly enough that your body does not totter. Knife-hand strikes to the spleen are done in this same way.

driving knife-hand strike to the collarbone

(shuto sakotsu-uchikomi)

If, for instance, your opponent has you by the collar, you can deliver a straight-line driving knife-hand strike to his collarbone. In this case, have a firm stance and a completely stable lower body.

upper elbow strike
(hiji jodan-ate)

Bend your elbow firmly, and with a spring in your hips strike from the outside inward to your opponent's face. Keep your withdrawn arm pulled in tight. Using the same basic elements, you can also strike to your opponent's abdomen.

rising elbow strike
(hiji age-uchi)

Using a method similar to what you use in the elbow strike, putting your whole body's counter forces into the blow, aim an elbow uppercut at your opponent's chin.

descending elbow strike

(hiji oroshi-uchi)

Squat and strike downward with your elbow.

CHAPTER 5 kicks

Kicks pack about five times as much destructive force as hand blows, and about 70% of all karate techniques use them. On the other hand, in comparison with the arms, the feet, though powerful, lack speed. In addition, since in all kicks except the flying kick one foot must remain on the floor for support, kicks are inferior in balance. Effective use of kicks demands that we give thought to ways to make up for these two deficiencies. If the body is out of balance, kicking techniques lose from 60%–70% of their power. Because your opponent can grab and hang on to your kicking leg if it lacks speed, slowness in these techniques can be fatal. The most important factor in the kicking techniques is to kick strong and fast and to snap your leg back the same way.

Keeping your body balanced always on a straight vertical line is important; that is, you must keep the upper half of your body and your supporting leg always in a straight line vertical to the floor. The kicking leg swings outward in a semicircle from this straight line. If you cannot kick this way, your body will lose its balance. If the upper half of your body inclines to the back in the kick, any force applied to you will be able easily to knock you over, and if your opponent grabs your kicking leg, you will be absolutely unable to get away from him. Moreover, even if your kick hits the mark, if half of your body's strength inclines to the rear, the power of your kick diminishes by half.

Leaning the top half of your body forward is just as bad, because then your face juts to the front and becomes an easy target for your opponent's attack. If the line of your body's center of gravity leans forward, the arc through which your kicking leg will travel decreases, and the power of your kick diminishes accordingly. In addition, you will lose your balance when you attempt to return your leg after a kick if the upper half of your body inclines forward. As we have already said, and as we shall repeat over and over, in karate balance and stability are of the utmost importance. To develop speed, balance is essential; to develop balance, speed is essential. The two are completely inseparable.

Make sure you understand these points thoroughly and that you apply them carefully when you practice kicks.

front kick ***(mae-geri)***

Kick to your opponent's abdomen with the ball of your foot. First put a good bend in the knee of the kicking leg, raise that knee as high as you can, keeping the lower part of the leg relaxed. Next snap the lower part of your leg out sharp and hard. The two main movements in the kick, then, are the bending and raising of the knee and the outward snap with the lower part of the leg, but when you actually kick you must perform the two together as one rapid movement. When you bring the kicking leg back, bend it first, then lower it, because this enables you to recover your leg quickly and without disturbing your body's balance. When you practice, each kick must be rapidly, but completely performed. Leave a one-second interval between kicks. Be careful not to let the heel of your supporting leg leave the floor while you kick.

high kick ***(keage)***

Aim at the opponent's head, and kick high with the ball of the foot. Be careful not to raise your heel so that you are standing on your toes because this will put you off balance. Be careful, also, of the position of your hands.

groin kick *(kin-geri)*

Just as in the preceding kick, first bend your knee. and using the knee as your fulcrum, kick out toward your opponent's groin with the instep of your foot. In the recovery, leaving your knee in the position it is in at the moment of the kick, first bring your foot back to you, then lower it to the floor. Once again. be sure that in both the kick and in the recovery you perform the two basic movements quickly as one. Practice carefully, kick after kick, and leave about a one-second interval between kicks.

knee kick ***(hiza-geri)***

We use the knee either to strike the opponent's abdomen or to drive into his face after we have grabbed his head and pulled it down into the striking range of the knee. Bend your knee way back, and thrust upward with the fleshy area above the kneecap. If your hips are out of balance in this technique the heel of the supporting foot will come off the floor. Be sure to tense your hips and keep steady. Be careful also that your upper body leans neither forward nor backward.

side high kick *(yoko-keage)*

In this side high kick to your opponent's chin you quickly and powerfully raise your knife foot to the side without bending the knee of the kicking leg. Be careful to keep your supporting leg as straight as you can and to avoid leaning your upper body to the side or to the back. Do not raise the heel of your supporting foot from the floor.

roundhouse kick ***(mawashi-geri)***

In this outside roundhouse kick with the ball of the foot to the opponent's upper body be sure that the supporting leg firmly maintains your body's balance. Bend the knee of your kicking leg, and raise it as high as you can. Using your knee as the fulcrum, keep the lower part of your leg parallel with the floor. Your foot should be at a diagonal with the floor. Twist your hips so that the ball of your kicking foot swings into your opponent.

2
1

roundhouse kick to the neck

(mawashi kubi-geri)

This kick to the throat and neck with the instep is performed exactly like the roundhouse kick, but the semicircular movement of the kicking foot is more effective the faster you perform it. Do not bend your support leg or your kicking leg.

side kick ***(yoko-geri)***

This straight-line kick to the side of the body's central line of balance is directed to the opponent's abdomen or neck. First bring the sole of your kicking foot to about the inside of the knee of the supporting leg, and then kick with knife foot straight out to the side. When you kick to the side, do it with the idea of a semicircle in mind. Always keep your big toe bent up as far as possible and your heel jutting outward so as to tighten the muscles in your foot.

ankle kick ***(kansetsu-geri)***

We use the ankle kick to strike at the opponent's knee from the front, back, or side. As in the side kick, we first raise the kicking foot to about the knee of the supporting leg and then, combining a snap in the kicking leg and a spring in the supporting one, kick outward. Keep the big toe of the kicking foot bent back and the heel jutting out.

heel kick *(kakato-geri)*

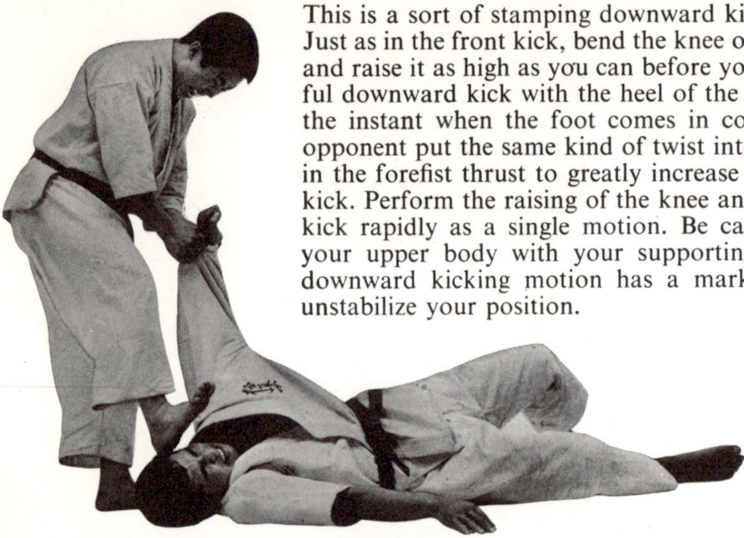

This is a sort of stamping downward kick with the heel. Just as in the front kick, bend the knee of the kicking leg, and raise it as high as you can before you drive a powerful downward kick with the heel of the kicking foot. At the instant when the foot comes in contact with your opponent put the same kind of twist into it that you use in the forefist thrust to greatly increase the effect of the kick. Perform the raising of the knee and the downward kick rapidly as a single motion. Be careful to balance your upper body with your supporting leg, since the downward kicking motion has a marked tendency to unstabilize your position.

back kick *(ushiro-geri)*

This kick serves in striking the abdomen of an opponent on whom your back is turned. The main points are similar to those in the roundhouse kick. First raise your leg, and then snap it straight back. Turn your heel inward at the instant of contact.

jumping front kick (***tobi-mae-geri***)

In this technique we are in the position for a front kick, but we jump as high as we can, and when we have reached the pinnacle of our jump, we kick with our ball of the foot to the opponent's face or neck. Since when you recover from the jump you can easily lose your balance, you must jump as high as you can. Be sure you bring the kicking foot back into your body before you land. Land as gently as possible on the tips of the toes of both feet. Jump from a standstill; do not make a preparatory run. The jumping side kick is done in the same way except that you kick to the side.

CHAPTER 6 blocks

As it is in other combat sports, blocking is an extremely vital phase of karate. The distinctive feature of the karate block is that, when properly executed, it leaves the defender in a good position to move to the attack. It has often been said that a good attack is the best defense. In karate, a good defense may also be the best attack. The two are opposite sides of the same coin. The expert blocker is also the expert attacker.

Basically, blocking movements should be round swinging movements. Straight movements in which the attacking blow is met at right angles are not necessarily wrong, but movements in which the limbs describe an arc are usually more effective.

forefist upper block *(seiken jodan-uke)*

We use the upper block against attacks to the face. We can use either the forefist or the knife hand; the main points and the forms are the same in both. Just as in the case of the thrust, it is vital to quickly and powerfully draw back the hand not used in the actual block so as to create a counter force that heightens the power and effect of the blocking hand.

It is extremely important to revolve the blocking arm.

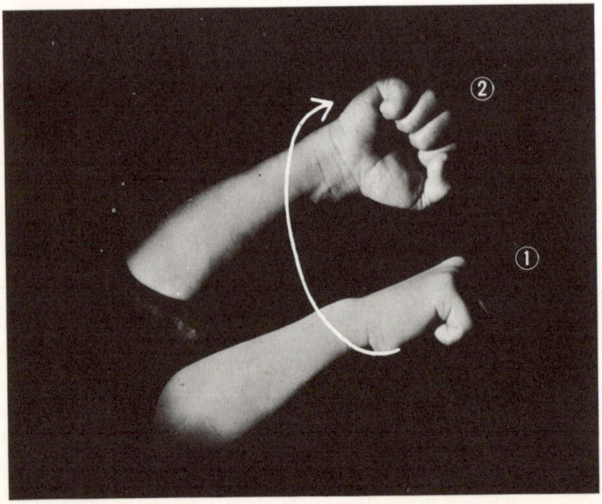

■ Attacker has aimed at the defender's head but has been blocked with an upper forearm block (left). In a block of this sort, the arm should not meet the attacking blow at right angles. If the angle of the arm is too small, the attack is successful (right).

forefist middle outside block

(seiken chudan soto-uke)

We use middle blocks against attacks to the body. We may block with either the forefist or with the knife hand. Whichever you use, put the hand of the blocking arm in front of your forehead and using that position as a control point block in front of your own body by swinging your elbow outside inward in a semicircular movement.

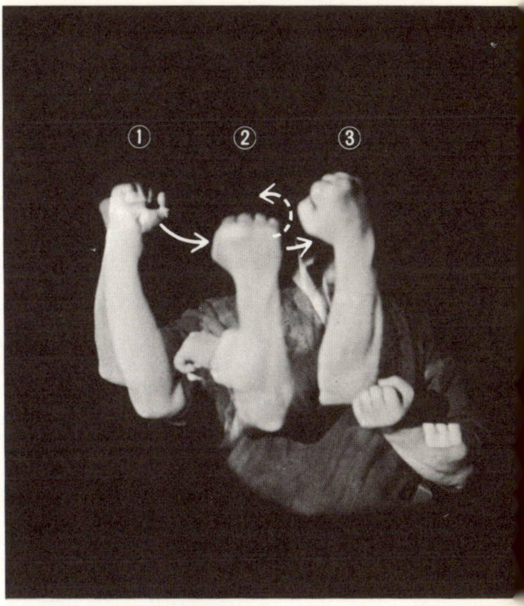

■ The attack is blocked with an outside forearm block (left). If the arm is not brought around in front of the body, the block fails (right).

forefist middle inside block
(seiken chudan uchi-uke)

The form and the main features are the same as those for the preceding block, and once again we use either the forefist or the knife hand. Keeping the blocking arm on the inside, cross one arm over the other in front of you. Beginning at about the armpit of the withdrawn arm swing the blocking arm outward in a large circle. It is important to turn your arm using the elbow as your control fulcrum. Of course, when you block your opponent's attack, put a twist in your blocking arm for extra strength. Keep your withdrawn arm tightly tensed.

■ Attacker has aimed at the chest and been blocked by a left inside block (left). If block is faulty, the arm is too far inside and attacker succeeds (right).

forefist lower parry *(seiken gedan-barai)*

We use this parry to fend off blows to the abdomen. The parrying arm swings downward from a position near the ear on the opposite side of the body. The twist in the parrying arm and the tensing of the withdrawn arm are the same as in all the other blocks.

■ The attacker has attempted to spear the defender's midriff but has been warded off with a left lower parry (left). The arm has described an arc, starting with the hand near the right side of the head and ending as shown. When the arm is too far inside, the attacker's thrust succeeds (right).

palm-heel lower block

(shotei gedan-uke)

When your opponent attacks with a knife or some other weapon of that sort it is best to stay as far away from him as possible while you block his attack. This is the block we use in such instances. There are both upper and lower versions; the lower one is used to parry kicks from the opponent's feet.

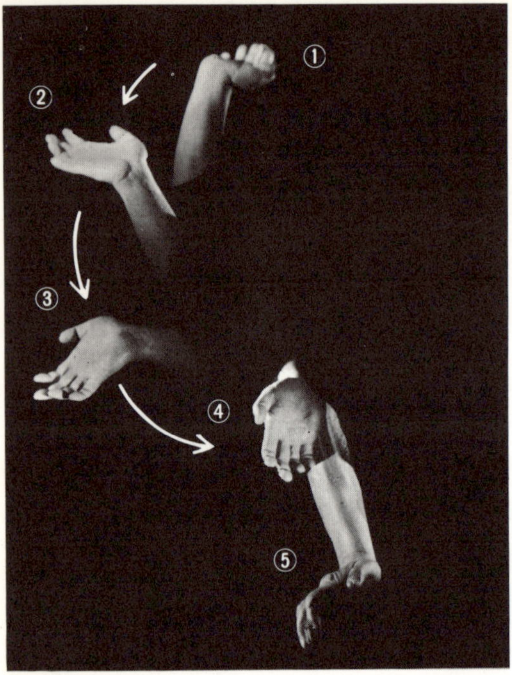
①
②
③
④
⑤

palm-heel middle outside block
(shotei chudan soto-uke)

palm-heel upper block
(shotei jodan-uke)

forefist middle inside block and low parry
(seiken chudan uchi-uke gedan-barai)

This is a combination of the two moves. When you cross your arms at your chest put your blocking hand on top.

■ Both arms are too far inside.

wrist middle inside block
(koken chudan uchi-uke)

Block with the wrist at the middle position, much as in the cases of the palm heel, except that the withdrawn hand is clenched in a forefist position.

the roundhouse block

Like the roundhouse strike, the knife-hand roundhouse block is one of the most important techniques and is a fundamental among the blocks. If we define karate as developing from points and circles, to which line is incidental, the roundhouse block is perfect illustrations. As we have said before, the block, centered on a point and describing a circle, is one of karate's greatest distinctions and is a great source of karate's interest.

1. Begin in a left back leaning stance, and make a circular motion from the groin.
2. Put both hands together, as in the photograph, and swing them to the right rear.
3. After you have made the circular motion, both hands will be behind your ear, from where you can prepare to fend the opponent's attack.
4. Preparing to execute a knife-hand block.
5. The left knife-hand block.

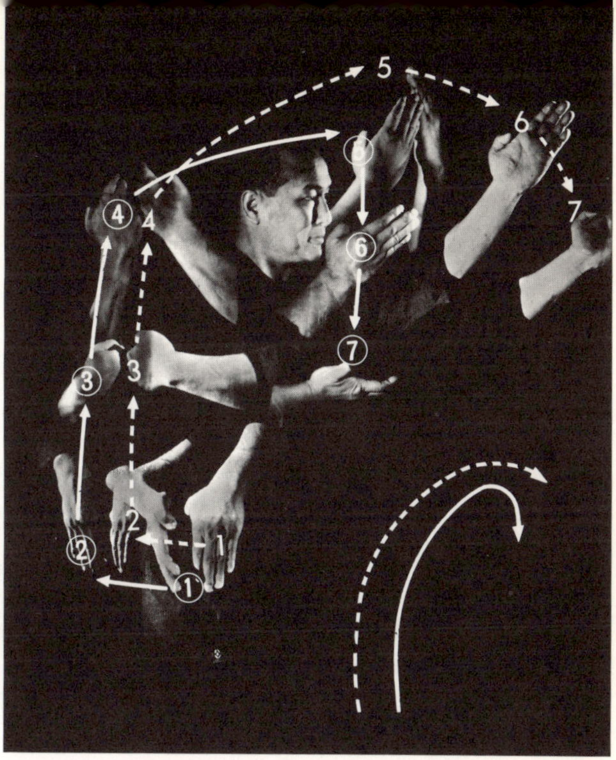

1. This is essentially the same as the block with the right hand, except that in this case the left hand is on the inside and the right hand is on the outside.
2. In both the right and the left blocks, begin at the central part of the body, the groin area, and bring the hands to the rear.
3. Join the backs of the hands as you make a circular movement.
4, 5. Open the hands behind the ear, and making a large semicircular motion, bring them to the front.
6. The left hand is to the front, and the right to the rear.
7. While blocking with the left hand, bring it to eye level. Block with a right knife hand so as to protect the waist area.

In either the right or left knife-hand round-house blocks, when you bring your hands together while making the circular motion, it is perfectly correct either to put one hand on top of the other or to join the backs of the hands.

CHAPTER **7**

practice fighting

The life of karate is formal practice fighting (*kumite*), without which karate is no more than a game for one person. Practice fighting is essential for the attainment of strength and skill.

Formal practice fighting is a mutual exchange of techniques. A great deal of practice is necessary in it to cultivate and to improve the speed of the eyes, hands, and feet. This type of work is genuinely useful and proves itself in actual combat. Neglecting this practice indicates a lack of understanding of the karate spirit.

To become proficient in formal practice fighting a thorough background and a great deal of practice in such basic techniques as the thrusts, strikes, kicks, and blocks is essential. The basic techniques in series make up the karate formal exercises, which in turn are the building blocks of practice fighting.

Although there are many types of formal practice fighting, they all fall roughly into three large categories: three-step, one-step and free-style practice fighting. In addition to these, there are also several specialized types, among which some involve the use of sticks, chains, and scythes. The beginner must first spend long hours on the three-step practice, which consists of basic movements repeated three times. When he has mastered this, he can go on to the more complicated one-step and free-style. Although there is a training regimen for any sport, karate is particularly demanding of constant practice to insure that you use the techniques to their best advantage.

three-step practice fighting

In three-step practice fighting (*sambon-kumite*) one person assumes the role of the attacker, and one that of the defender. The attacker, using the same technique each time, attacks three times (a lunge technique), and the defender, also using the same technique each time, blocks all three attacks (a lunge block). At the conclusion of the third block, the defender adds a counter-attack. The movements involved are the attacking technique, the defensive blocking technique, the counter-attack technique, and the proper footwork.

1 ■ The attacker delivers a right forefist middle thrust. (Note: In the first step of the fight the right hand performs the thrust, in the second step the left, in the third step the right, or *vice versa.* This is true of both the attack and the defense techniques.)

■ The defender blocks with a left middle outside block with the forefist and counter-attacks with a right forefist middle thrust to the ribs.

■ Before the fight begins, both opponents bow, and as the defender counter-attacks, he shouts. This is true throughout all the practice fighting forms.

■ An adaptation of step one calls for the same attack but for a defense with an inside block and a counter-attack with a left middle forefist thrust to the pit of the stomach.

2 ■ The attack is as in 1.
■ The defender blocks with a middle outside block with his right forefist and counter-attacks with a strike to the face with a right inverted fist. In this case the blocking hand also performs the counter-attack.
■ An adaptation calls for the same attack and a defense with the inside block and a counter-attack with left forefist middle strike to the ribs.

3 ■ The attacker delivers an upper right forefist strike.
■ The defender blocks with a left forefist upper block and counter-attacks with a right upper forefist strike to the face.
■ An adaptation calls for the same attack, a right forefist upper block, and a counter-attack with a right fist-edge strike to the ribs.

4

- The attacker delivers an upper left forefist strike.
- The defender blocks with an upper left forefist inside block and counter-attacks with a left forefist middle strike to the ribs.

5

- The attacker delivers a right forefist middle thrust.
- The defender blocks with a left palm-heel middle outside block and counter-attacks with a right inner knife-hand strike to the stomach.
- An adaptation calls for the same attack, a defense with the right outside block, and a counter-attack with a right knife-hand strike to the ribs.
- Another adaptation calls for the same attack, a defense with a left inner knife-hand middle inside block, and a counter-attack with a right knife-hand strike to the solar plexus.

6 ▪ The attack is the same as in 5.
▪ The defender blocks with a right inner knife-hand

7 ▪ The attacker delivers a right forefist upper strike.
▪ The defender blocks with a left knife-hand upper inside block and counter-attacks with a right knife-hand strike to the face.

8 ▪ The attack is the same as in 7
▪ The defender blocks with a right knife-hand upper in-

middle inside block and counter-attacks with a left knife-hand strike to the ribs.

■ An adaptation calls for the same attack, a defense with a right knife-hand upper inside block, and a counter-attack with a left knife-hand strike to the ribs.

side block and counter-attacks with a right knife-hand strike to the ribs.

one-step practice fighting

Fundamentally, there is little difference between three-step practice fighting and one-step practice fighting. The former consists of exercises in which three attacks are met by three blocks and one counter-attack, while the latter consists of one attack met by one block and counter-attack. In general, the movements employed in three-step practice fighting are the simpler and more basic. A beginner must first master three-step practice and then go on to the subtler one-step practice.

One point of difference between the two types is that in three-step practice fighting the fist is often kept closed, whereas in one-step practice the hand is always open. In effect, however, one-step practice fighting is simply a more advanced form.

A good beginning stance for one-step practice fighting is the half straddle stance, with the feet at about 45 degrees. Dependent on the fighters' sizes and their relative heights, it may be advantageous to choose another stance—forward, rear, or full straddle—but the half straddle stance is, on the whole, the safest.

1 a. Attacker (left) assumes forward leaning stance; defender is in half straddle stance.
b. Attacker makes a right forefist middle thrust, which is met with a right middle wrist block.
c. Defender follows through with a palm-heel strike to attacker's solar plexus.

beginning stance

2

a. Beginning stance is as before. Attacker makes a right middle forefist thrust, which is met by a left knife-hand block.
b. Defender forces attacker's right arm outward.
c. Defender delivers a right knife-hand strike to attacker's solar plexus.

3

a. Beginning stance is as before. Attacker makes a right forefist middle thrust, which is met by a right palm-heel block.
b. With blocking arm, defender pushes attacker's right arm aside.
c. Defender immediately delivers a right knife-hand strike to attacker's right jaw.

beginning stance

4

a. Beginning stance is as in 1.
b. Attacker makes a right upper thrust, which is met by a left knife-hand block. Defender should keep his own arms apart and should place his left foot as close as possible to attacker's right foot.
c. Defender delivers a right spear-hand strike to attacker's eyes as agilely as possible.

5

a-b. The same as before.
c. Defender delivers a right palm-heel strike to attacker's solar plexus.

beginning stance

6 a. Beginning stance is as before.
b. Attacker makes a right upper thrust which is met with a right knife-hand block.
c. Defender delivers a right knife-hand strike to attacker's ribs. In making this strike, defender moves his right leg forward so that it is between attacker's legs.

7 a. Attacker makes a right upper thrust which is met with a right knife-hand block.
b. With this blocking hand, defender obtains a *tensho* cover on the attacker's wrist and brings his left hand to the back of attacker's elbow. At the same time, defender steps forward so that his left foot is against the inner side of attacker's right foot.
c. As the defender gets his leg inside the attacker's, he pulls up on attacker's wrist with his right hand and presses down on attacker's elbow with his left hand. (Defender's left foot trips attacker.) This is a good way to break the attacker's arm.

8

a. Beginning stance is as before. Attacker makes a right upper forefist thrust which is met with a left upper knife-hand inside block.

b. With blocking hand, the defender gets an outside *tensho* cover on the attacker's wrist, at the same time striking attacker's temple with a right knife-hand.

9 a. Attacker makes a right middle thrust, which is met with a right knife-hand reverse outer block.
b. Defender quickly steps around attacker, placing his right leg behind attacker's right (forward) leg. At the same time, defender follows through on the blocking swing, wrapping his right arm around attacker's arm from underneath.
c-d. Defender brings his right foot from behind and trips attacker, at the same time pushing attacker over with his right hand.

10 a. Attacker makes a right middle thrust which is met with a left middle knife-hand downward block.
b. While blocking, defender moves rapidly in and grasps attacker's genitals with his right hand.
c. Defender's blocking hand describes an arc in forcing attacker's right hand aside. Defender simultaneously pulls attacker's crotch forward.
d. Seen from the opposite side.

11 a. When attacker attempts a right middle thrust defender seizes the wrist of the attacking arm with both hands.
b. Defender twists attacker's wrist, bringing the underside up.
c. Defender pushes forward and downward with both hands, bringing attacker to his knees.

CHAPTER

8 self-defense techniques

As I have said many times, a karate man's daily spiritual attitude is most important because he must, as far as is possible, always avoid conflict. This is one of the first rules of karate. Karate daily training is designed to help us avoid individual fights.

The fact remains, however, that as society grows more complex, everyday and everywhere we hear more tales of violence and of infringements of social morality. Because we have no idea when we might ourselves run into a person bent on evil, we cannot afford to be negligent even in our intimate daily activities. To this end we need self-defense techniques, because the spiritual attitudes themselves of people who do and of those who do not know how to defend themselves are very different. A man who knows and understands how to protect himself can always maintain a natural spiritual attitude which reflects in his approach to daily life. Though he will not give an opponent chances to attack him, since he never encounters danger except when it is necessary to do so, the likelihood of his running into trouble is less than it is with a person who cannot take care of himself.

From the viewpoint that self-defense techniques are a vital element of the martial arts, I firmly believe in their indispensability, but if your opponent attacks you and you feel yourself in danger you must also be able to confidently use the techniques you practice everyday at the training hall. At the moment of crisis, the most important thing in self-defense is to keep cool. Your opponent, in a similar situation, is likely to lose control of himself, and if you simply watch what he does and how he moves you will be able to find the weak spot in his technique. For this reason, in daily practice always aim for calm, speed, and accurate application of techniques.

Though the self-defense techniques we include in this chapter are basic and easy to use and learn, they are extremely effective. Limitations in the size of the book have made it impossible to introduce as many techniques as we should like to, but be sure you learn these few thoroughly.

one against two

What is the best thing to do to get away from a number of opponents who have you by the wrists or the arms? If your opponents are unarmed, you can get away quite easily from about four people. If five or more have ganged up on you, the escape methods are somewhat different. We have introduced here the very basic karate technique for use against two opponents.

1. One opponent has you by both upper arms from the rear while another has you by one lapel and is about to strike you.
2. Raise both elbows and thrust to the rear opponent's solar plexus. When the rear opponent is off balance, cover your chin to protect it from the front opponent's blow.
3. While taking one step forward on your right foot, swing your left foot 180 degrees to the left. Without changing the position of your upper body, strike the front opponent in the solar plexus.
4. In the next instant, kick your rear opponent in the groin with your left foot.
5. Next strike him in the chin with your right elbow, and he will fall.

1. Opponents have you by the right and the left wrists.
2. Pivot on your left foot, twist your body, and kick your left opponent in the left armpit with a right roundhouse kick. In this case, do not tense the captured hand.
3. With your right leg, with which you have just kicked the left opponent, make a continuous movement to the rear,and aim a deliberate side kick at the right opponent's solar plexus.
4. Immediately after you lower your left foot, drive your left elbow into the right opponent's solar plexus.
5. Quickly aim a high right side kick at the left opponent's neck or chin.

1. Opponents have seized you from front and back. The front opponent has you by both lapels, and the rear opponent by both elbows.

2. Raise both arms and knock off both wrists of the opponent in the rear. Bring both elbows down in a crushing blow, and strike the elbow joints of the front opponent with all your might.

3. When the front opponent is off balance, strike him in the chin with your right elbow.

4. At the instant the front opponent falls back, strike the rear opponent in the solar plexus with your right elbow.

5. As the rear opponent falls forward, shake yourself free.

self-defense for women

A woman who knows something of how to defend herself in a crisis is much better off than the woman who does not and who first tries to run away, because flight is often the best way to fall into your enemy's hands. A man who attacks a woman is sure to be stronger than his victim, but if the women will calmly apply the principles of the point and circle, which we explained earlier, and will learn the following few techniques, she will always be able to get away from any masher. In training you should first study and learn all of the body movements and leg actions slowly together and then try adding speed to them.

1. Your attacker has grabbed you by one hand from behind (in this case the right hand). Absolutely do not attempt to move forward because in instances of this sort the arm doing the holding is stronger in backward and forward motions.
2. Close your arm tightly keeping it close to your body, and as you pivot on your right foot 180 degrees in a clockwise direction, tense the fourth and little fingers of your right hand, and bring it down on top of your opponent's hand. Simultaneously, bring your left hand around on top of your opponent's hand, and immobilize it.
3. Bring your left elbow down on top of your opponent's already covered hand, and press up on it from below. Make sure that this action makes it impossible for your opponent to withdraw his hand.
4. Now that you have a reverse hold on your opponent's arm, should he stoop forward, kick up into his face.

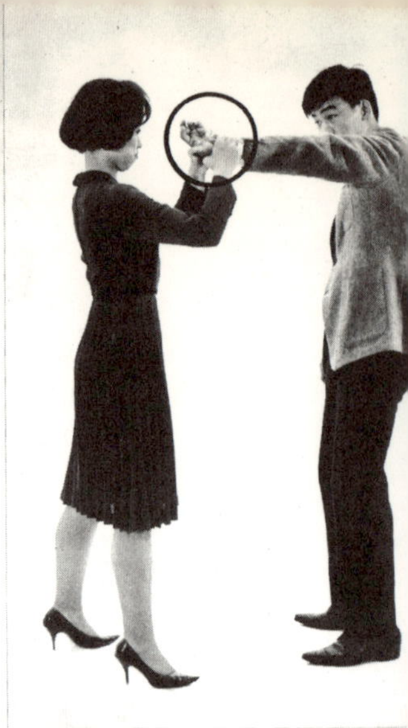

1. Your attacker has you by one hand (in this case the right hand). Be sure you are calm and that you tense your abdomen and keep your body in good balance.
2. Raise the captive hand, and describing a circle from the outside to the inside (counterclockwise direction), seize your

1. The man has seized the girl's right hand in his left hand.
2. Suddenly open your right arm which the man is holding, stiffen the fingertips of that hand, and thrust upward into the man's left armpit. Take one step with your right foot, and turn your body half way to the left.
3. Twist your right arm into the man's left arm, and holding

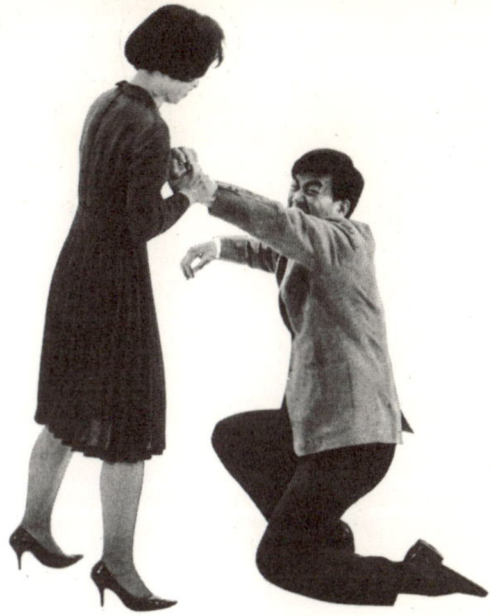

opponent's wrist between your thumb and your index finger.
3. Bring your free hand around to the back of your opponent's hand, and get a firm hold on his wrist.
4. Bend his wrist severely by twisting it hard inward and by bending it down.

your handbag, with both hands twist the man's left shoulder joint.
4. Stiffen your right arm which is holding the man's shoulder joint and pull it downwards to the left. At the same time, strike the man in the face with your left knee. Do not release your handbag.

1. The man is about to strike with the knife. In this instance cover either your breast or your groin area with your handbag.
2. At the instant of the blow, turn your body half to the right and let the handbag receive the stab. You should be holding the handbag in your right hand.
3. In the next instant seize the man's right wrist with your left hand and raise it. The movement must be executed speedily.

1. The man has grabbed the woman's left wrist from behind.
2. Pivoting on your right foot, turn your body half way to the left, and kick the outside of the man's right leg with all your strength. At the same time raise the left hand, which the man is holding, as far as possible while drawing back your right hand, in which you hold your handbag.

4. While placing your right foot in front of the man's right foot, release your handbag and rapidly twist your arm under the man's armpit, and bend his elbow back. While holding tightly with your right arm, which is twisting the man's elbow, press downward with your left hand, which is holding the man's elbow.

3. Turning toward the man, strike him in the face with your handbag.
4. When the force of the man's body is broken, immediately strike the back of his right knee with your right foot and press downward. At the same time, apply strong pressure to the handbag which you have held against his face.

1. Always make full use of a parasol or any other accessory you might have with you when an attacker approaches. In this case, the opponent has grabbed one of your hands (the left in the photograph) from the front. Always switch the parasol to the captive hand.
2. Swing the handle of the parasol to the outside.
3. Swing the handle around on top of the opponent's wrist, and grip farther up on the handle with your free hand.
4. Bend your attacker's wrist by giving a sharp downward tug on the parasol handle.

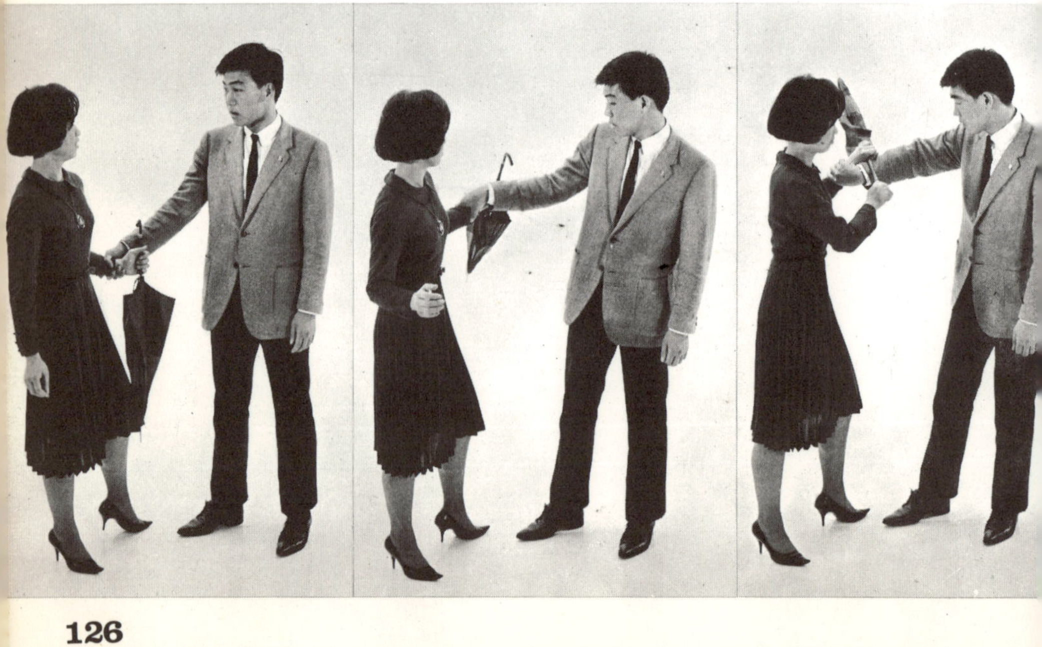

1. Should a masher put both arms around you and attempt to cover your mouth from behind, the first thing to do is stay calm.
2. Thrust the handle of your parasol into your attacker's throat.
3. When he flinches, thrust with your elbow into his stomach.
4. If you thrust again with the parasol into his throat you can get free.

1. Your attacker has you by both hands from behind.
2. Quickly open both arms to the outside, and take a step back on your left foot outside your opponent's right foot. This is an effective action because the person being held is stronger in motions to the right and left than in motions to front or back.
3. Duck back under your opponent's arm, pull your right hand back, and apply heavy pressure to his elbow with your left hand to reverse the hand hold he had on you.
4. Bend his elbow by pressing hard and firm into it with a left knife hand from above. Naturally, you must perform motions 1, 2, and 3 rapidly without letting go of your opponent's hands.